[LET US MARCH ON! SELECTED CIVIL RIGHTS PHOTOGRAPHS OF ERNEST C. WITHERS 1955-1968]

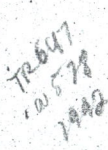

Let Us March On! Selected Civil Rights Photographs of Ernest C. Withers 1955-1968

Organized by the Massachusetts College of Art and the Department of African-American Studies,
Northeastern University, Boston, Massachusetts

88 pages, 21.5 cm

Published in conjunction with an exhibition at the Massachusetts College of Art,
November 9 -December 19, 1992

Edited by Ronald W. Bailey and Michèle Furst
Preface by Margaret Walker

Distributed by: Massachusetts College of Art
          621 Huntington Avenue, Boston, MA 02115
   and: The Afro Scholar Press
          PO Box 190747, Roxbury, MA 02119

ISBN 0-9628905-1-0 (paperback) and ISBN 0-942373-02-2 (paperback)
ISBN 0-9628905-2-9 (hard cover) and ISBN 0-942373-03-0 (hard cover)

© 1992 Massachusetts College of Art and Northeastern University

Project Directors:
   Ronald W. Bailey
   Michèle Furst
Curator:
   Michèle Furst
Administrative Assistant:
   Rosemary Williams
Director of Exhibitions:
   Jeffrey Keough
Preparator:
   Kay Rhynus
Friends:
   Tony Decaneas
   Ruth Ellis
   Mario Gomez
   Marjorie Hellerstein
   Margot Isabelle
   Shirrie Jenkins
   Laura Lakeway
   Abe Morell
   John O'Connell
   Michael St. Germain
   Steve Tourlentes
Supporters:
   Massachusetts College of Art
   Foundation, Inc.

   Massachusetts Foundation for
   the Humanities

   PANOPTICON, INC.
   Monadnock Paper Mills, Inc.
   Ilford Photo Corporation
   Metalwoods Workshop, Inc.

ACKNOWLEDGEMENTS

In 1991 Ronald W. Bailey, Chair of the African-American Studies Department at Northeastern University, proposed that the Massachusetts College of Art collaborate in organizing major retrospective exhibition of Ernest Withers' civil rights photographs. As neighbors on Huntington Avenue in Boston, a partnership between the institutions seemed natural.

Both institutions provided support, resources and expertise. Rosemary Williams, Administrative Assistant for the Department of African-American Studies at Northeastern, was instrumental in the development of the project. Abe Morell, Chair of the Media and Performing Arts Department at Mass Art, provided curatorial assistance. Christy Park, Abigail Housen and the Art Education Department trained the docents who guided schoolchildren through the exhibition. Marjorie Hellerstein provided editorial assistance. Jeffrey Keough, Director of Exhibitions, designed the exhibition and gave crucial advice and support throughout.

The Massachusetts Foundation for the Humanities, a state program of the National Endowment for the Humanities, supported this exhibition catalogue. Panopticon, Inc. donated the beautiful exhibition prints, made by Mario Gomez; Tony Decaneas and Laura Lakeway of that organization supported the project from its earliest stages. Ilford Photo Corporation generously supplied photographic paper and Monadnock Paper Mills, Inc. supplied paper for this catalogue.

Most importantly, we thank Ernest C. Withers and his wife Dorothy, who gave generously of their time and memories and provided the inspiration for the exhibition.

Foreword, *by Margaret Walker*   2

Introduction, *by Michèle Furst*   4

Picturing the Black Experience
and Framing the Civil Rights
Photography of Ernest C. Withers
by Ronald W. Bailey   10

....

The Emmett Till Murder Trial
   Sumner, Mississippi, 1955   25

School Desegregation
   Little Rock, Arkansas, 1957   33

Memphis, Tennessee
   in the 1950s and 60s   37

Voter Registration
and the Tent City Protest
   Fayette County, Tennessee, 1960   45

James Meredith and the Mississippi
Campaign, *1962 and 1966*   49

Medgar Evers, *1925-1963*   57

Montgomery Bus Boycott
   Montgomery, Alabama, 1955   61

Sanitation Workers' Strike
   Memphis, Tennessee, 1968   65

Assassination of Dr. Martin Luther
King, Jr.,
   Memphis, Tennessee,
   April 4, 1968   71

Poor People's Campaign
   Marks, Mississippi and Washington,
   DC, 1968   79

....

Afterword, *by Ronald W. Bailey*   83

Bibliography   85

Meeting at Metropolitan Baptist Church, Memphis, TN, 1960. Rear: Unknown, Aaron Henry, Wade Walton, Attorney Carsie Hall. Front: H.Y. Hackett, Cleo Jackson, Medgar Evers, John Melchoir.

THE PHOTOGRAPHS OF Ernest C. Withers of Memphis, Tennessee are a valuable educational and cultural resource. I am happy to write this brief comment to applaud his work, and the effort to develop this exhibition and catalogue. As we struggle to grapple with the history, contemporary strains, and the future prospects of the relations between Black people and the American social order, these photographs must be judged as an important contribution.

The real strength of the Civil Rights Movement in the 1950s and 1960s was the thousands of men and women who rallied to the cause of justice, who put their lives on the line to do the right thing. Ernest Withers was certainly one of them. He was an integral component in the machinery of the civil rights struggle. And he has produced a very eloquent and passionate body of testimony—the thousands of photographic images from which the hundred and twenty-two in this exhibition were selected.

HE WAS THERE!!!! And he was there in a way which distinguishes him as an important contributor to the movement, and as a key contributor to the knowledge about the workings of this decisive struggle to future generations. I am sure that the many civil rights partisans we see in these photographs were very pleased to see that Ernest Withers

Foreword

was there using his intellect and his skills to spread the word about the struggle.

I see so much of my own personal history and the history which shaped me, the South and the U.S. in these photographs. The trials and tribulations of the Civil Rights Movement, and its many victories, are reflected in much of my poetry. The killing of Emmett Till shocked the world and started a new stage in the Movement. By the time President Kennedy was assasinated in November 1963, there had been many brutal killings in the South. Our neighbor Medgar Evers was assassinated on the street where I still live. Four little girls were killed when Sixteenth Street Baptist Church in Birmingham was bombed. One of those children was the granddaughter of a neighbor from my childhood days in Birmingham, and he took me to worship in that church. I gradually came to know many of the civil rights leaders, men and women, and I was moved to write my civil rights poems in 1963, the poems in my book, *Prophets for a New Day*.

These photographs of Ernest Withers put before us the same kinds of images I wanted to capture in my poetry—images of men and women fighting together as leaders and activists in local and national struggles. The crowd images in Mr. Withers' collection remind us of the important lesson that the Civil Rights Movement—indeed, no social movement—is comprised only of the work of great men and women. Successful social movements are based on the masses of people. I am also very pleased to see the many photographs of Black women who were key and too often unheralded participants in the Civil Rights Movement.

Contrary to the views of some people, the importance of the Civil Rights Movement is not just a consideration for the history textbooks. As I complete work on this essay and as this exhibit is being prepared, there are significant legacies of the civil rights struggle still unfolding. For example, there is the possibility of a third trial of Byron de La Beckwith. Beckwith was twice found innocent on charges that he murdered Medgar Evers, even though his prints were on the murder weapon found in a field across from the Evers' home. Because of evidence that there was significant jury tampering, Beckwith has been held in a Mississippi jail and the final decision and a schedule for this trial will hopefully come very soon. And this time, we can only pray that justice will be done.

The photographs of Ernest Withers remind us that the movement for social justice and social transformation is not over. Progress has been made. Black men and women have been elected to local, state and federal offices, and others hold key jobs throughout the private sector.

These photographs also speak to us about the deeper causes of the Civil Rights Movement—continuing poverty, discrimination, and oppression. These were the real conditions that the Civil Rights Movement set out to change. These changes are as necessary today as they were in the 1950s and 1960s, though we must constantly update our understanding of the problems and the conditions we face in the 1990s.

Just as Ernest Withers has not yet put down his camera after fifty years, we too must not waiver in our commitment to justice for all. As we approach the 21st century, let these photographs of Ernest Withers spur us onwards and upwards "'til victory is won!"

Dr. Margaret Walker
Jackson, Mississippi

Dr. Margaret Walker is Professor Emeritus at Jackson State University in Mississippi. She is the author of For My People, *which won the Yale University Younger Poets Award in 1942, the historical novel* Jubilee *(1976),* Richard Wright: Daemonic Genius *(1988),* This is My Century: New and Collected Poems *(1989),* How I Wrote Jubilee and Other Essays on Life and Literature *(1990) and other books.*

FIGURE 2. *Ernest C. Withers*

Introduction

Ernest C. Withers has been making photographs for almost sixty years [2]. His subjects are individuals and groups and the events which they create for themselves — the celebrations, social events, political gatherings and groupings that are the mile markers of personal and group histories.

This exhibition of more than one hundred photographs is the first extensive presentation and publication of Withers' work documenting the Civil Rights Movement in the American South.

Withers' very particular point of view is informed by his personal history, that of a socially conscious citizen who worked hard to support his community and raise a family of eight children in Memphis, his home town and a city which was segregated until the 1960s. In 1955, a photograph of the mutilated body of fourteen year old Emmett Till, published in *Jet* Magazine, shocked Black communities throughout the U.S. Ernest Withers' identification as a civil rights photographer began with his coverage of the ensuing trial of two white men (and their acquittal by an all white male jury) for the murder of Emmett Till.

In a few important ways, Withers must be distinguished from other photojournalists who covered the people and events of the Civil Rights Movement. First, Withers, unlike some of the Northern and/or white photojournalists covering the South, was a participant in the Movement, not just an observer. He regularly received phone calls from activists and organizations to alert him to current and future actions. Withers saw his work as a contribution to the movement for social change, and, therefore, his role was that of social documentarian, a recorder of real people engaged in important activities, participating in historic events. Second, he was often unpaid for his work, although paid assignments were done for the *Tri-State Defender* and *Chicago Defender*. Early in the 1950s, Withers worked with a 4"x5" Speed Graphic, a large camera and flash unit which made him highly visible and sometimes vulnerable. He later switched to a 120 Flexinet, a more convenient and less conspicuous format.

It was clear from the start of his coverage of the Civil Rights Movement that Withers' intention was not merely to document events. Like many activists, Withers believed that if the struggle for equality could be shown, people would surely move to change the way things were. In a single-minded effort to get out the pictures quickly, Withers sometimes, during a critical demonstration or event, would sell a roll of exposed film on the spot to an out-of-town journalist, just to be sure the pictures would be published. His photos were widely used (in *Time, Life, Newsweek*) and often uncredited.

When there was no ready outlet for publication, Withers created his own. In 1955 he self-published a small, inexpensively printed book of text and photographs (reprinted in this catalogue) after the trial of the accused murderers of Emmett Till. The by-line on the pamphlet reads, "*Authentic pictures taken on the spot, designed to meet public demand. Complete photo story of Till Murder Case; 1st and only complete factual photo story of Till Case.*" It was sold throughout the South for $1.00.

The hundreds of images compiled by Ernest Withers during the civil rights years make tangible a sense of the scale and consistency of the Movement. Through examination of Withers' massive archives, the Civil Rights Movement in the South in the 1950s and 60s reveals itself as a major conflict, waged with serious intent by many people in many places, over a long period of time. Withers' photos testify to the courage and commitment of thousands of Americans confronted by the savage hostility of thousands of others. It is remarkable that all of these images were recorded by one man, often working alone, without enormous resources. Furthermore, Withers was based in Memphis, main-

FIGURE 3

FIGURE 4

FIGURE 5

taining his photographic studio, and only able to travel for short periods.

The intent of this exhibition is neither to present documents of all of the events and people of the Civil Rights Movement, nor to offer a complete record of all that Withers photographed. Rather, it is to present a selection, a sample of images, which illuminate the finely tuned humanistic vision which informed Ernest Withers' obsession to document.

At least four major themes recur throughout the exhibition. First, there are numerous images of violent conflict: National Guard troops block a street ; marchers stand in linked-arm formation shattered streets and buildings; wounded bodies and many funerals The deaths of civilians, some famous, some not, confirm that violence and grief were nearly constant.

Next, Withers documents the strength of leadership, in portraits and action photos of the men and women in many communities who were great organizers and strategists. A photograph of Dr. Martin Luther King, Jr. and other Movement leaders during the 1966 *March Against Fear* shows the group seated in a church basement, carrying on an intense discussion as sunlight streams through windows high up on the walls. The image resonates with the power of thoughtful, determined leadership. A striking photograph of Mrs. Maxine Smith shows the Memphis NAACP leader striding down the sidewalk, her head held high, her companions struggling to keep up

A third theme is a "behind-the-scenes" view of preparations, actions and their aftermath. A particularly moving sequence of photographs shows James Meredith (the first Black student to enter the University of Mississippi at Oxford, in 1962) preparing to rejoin his "*March Against Fear*" in 1966 Meredith had planned to walk across the South to prove that a Black man could do so without fear; he was shot on the second day of his walk. Dr. Martin Luther King Jr., James Farmer, Stokely Carmichael and hundreds of others then joined the march. Meredith's departure is framed by tender goodbyes to his mother and female relatives, who have baked him a cake.

The fourth major theme is the impact of printed communication via placards and signs. Organizers demonstrated a knowledge of the importance of visual statements as transmitted by the print and electronic media. Withers recorded the official signage of segregation and the creative signs men, women and children carried proudly and bravely against it. The sign on the Memphis Zoo in

FIGURE 6

FIGURE 7

FIGURE 8

FIGURE 9

Overton Park ⑨, "*No White People Allowed in Zoo Today*" startles the viewer into understanding that segregation was apartheid. Just one day a week was reserved for Blacks only, an unequal separation of the races by statute.

In several of these images of individuals with their placards, Withers displays his enjoyment of contradictory visual messages. In one, a man pushing his baby in a stroller is being hassled by the police in a patrol car. The baby is holding a sign proclaiming, "*Daddy I Want To Be Free*" ⑩. In another image, a single, tired-looking man walks slowly home as he is passed by a truck loaded with armed National Guardsmen. His sign reads "*We Are All Together*" ⑪.

A sub-theme emerges from Withers' deep understanding of the complex role of the press and photographers in the Movement. There are many photos of the press at work: reporters type in the Press Room at "Ole Miss" (it was an integrated part of campus) ⑫; a photographer takes a light meter reading on the recently slain Dr. Martin Luther King, Jr. in a Memphis funeral home ⑬; Ernestine Cofield, reporter for the *Tri-State Defender*, interviews the motel waitress who served Dr. King his last meal, and an open truck loaded with photojournalists sets forth with an amused local child hanging off the back ⑭.

Withers also displays a fine touch in capturing moments of perfect grace, in his portraits of individuals at peace with themselves and their actions. While the majority of Withers' images are of movement, energy and determination, a few posed photographs depict rare instances of stillness, split-seconds away from the fray. Photographs taken in 1960 at Tent City in Fayette County, Tennessee (set up when families were evicted from their homes for voting) are portraits of proud, cohesive families. An earlier Memphis photograph freezes a group of lovely young women in full-skirted party and church dresses as they leap gracefully, political signs held high, down a hillside to the road. A perfect mid-summer sky provides the backdrop ⑮.

To a contemporary audience, these images may not seem dated at all. These are the kinds of images which we may, and do, see in newspapers and on television. For Withers the social documentarian, content was always the motivating factor. He obsessively recorded events and people involved in activities they may not have imagined possible before.

Not unlike the works of photographer Lewis Hine, who in 1940 described his work as, "Ever the Human Document - to keep the present and future in touch with the past,"[1] Withers' photographs allow us to reflect on what the Civil

Rights Movement still means today and what its future will require of us.

The Massachusetts College of Art and the African-American Studies Department of Northeastern University are privileged to present this selection of the civil rights photographs of Ernest C. Withers. These images were originally reproduced in newspapers and journals, interspersed with all the news of the day. By showing them together and in larger format, we hope to frame the images as Withers did and to glimpse him as both observer and operator. Withers' photographs are an important primary source; in conjunction with the notes and stories of their maker, they constitute an invaluable archive of the history of the Civil Rights Movement in the American South. The optimistic vision and generous spirit of Ernest Withers were the inspiration for the title of the exhibition, "*Let us March On!,*" referring to James Weldon Johnson's exhortation in the Negro National Anthem, "*Lift Every Voice and Sing.*"

Michèle Furst
Massachusetts College of Art

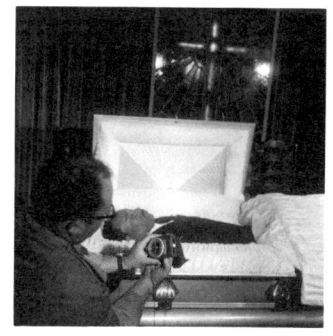

---

[1] *(quoted in* America and Lewis Hine, Photographs 1904-1940, *catalogue essay by Alan Trachtenberg, p. 118, Aperture, Inc., NY, 1977.)*

FIGURE 10

FIGURE 13

FIGURE 11

FIGURE 14

FIGURE 12

FIGURE 15

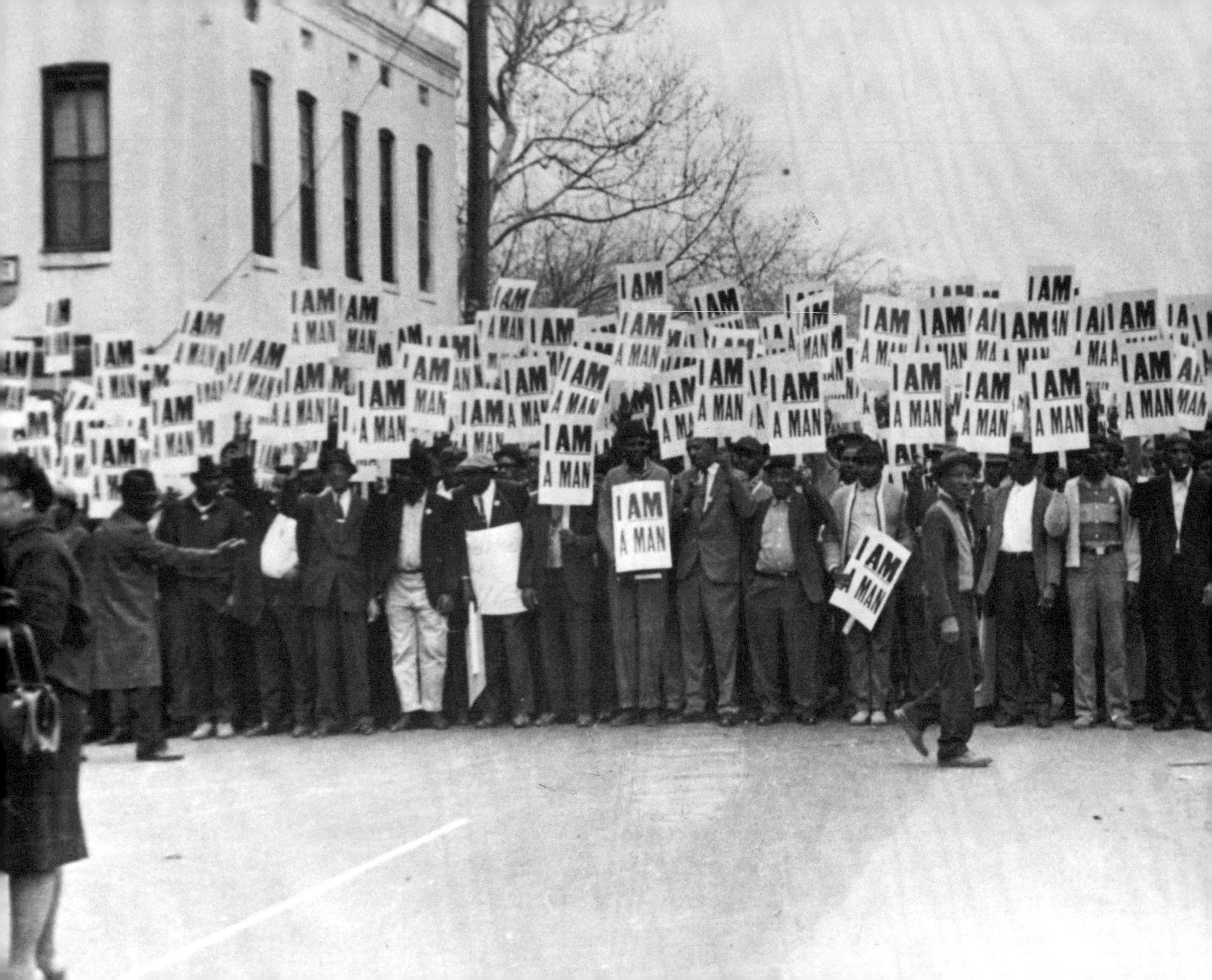
I AM
A MAN

PICTURING THE BLACK EXPERIENCE AND FRAMING THE CIVIL RIGHTS PHOTOGRAPHY OF ERNEST C. WITHERS[1]

IN 1991, I PROPOSED that the Massachusetts College of Art in collaboration with the Department of African-American Studies at Northeastern University bring Ernest C. Withers to Boston. Michèle Furst, Director of the College's Visiting Artists Program, responded enthusiastically. I have worked closely with her in shaping the project, and I am pleased to write this essay for the exhibit and catalogue featuring the work of Mr. Withers, a Memphis-based photographer whose timely photographs are a cornerstone of civil rights history.

As an amateur photographer who once took his photos very seriously, I have become particularly concerned about the lack of attention paid to the work of Black photographers, especially as I have seen repeated mention of the 150th anniversary of photography celebrated in 1989.[2] And as a scholar of the Black experience in the U.S., I am also deeply interested in the intellectual history of Black people—our efforts to chronicle and document our own stories about our lives, a principal mandate of the field of Black Studies. These two concerns come together in this project on the life and work of Ernest Withers.

I was frankly appalled at the meager efforts to recognize the contributions made by Black journalists and by Black photographers who did much of the necessary field work in fueling and documenting the Civil Rights Movement, but who saw much of the credit go to the national news media. "*Let Us March On! Civil Rights Photographs of Ernest C. Withers*" was the original title of a smaller exhibition of Mr. Withers' photographs presented at the University of Mississippi on April 3, 1987. It was organized to commemorate Dr. Martin Luther King, Jr., in conjunction with a major conference on campus, "*Civil Rights and the Mass Media*." The conference was timed to recognize the efforts to desegregate "Ole Miss" in 1962.[3] Ironically, the occasion marked a homecoming for Mr. Withers, who visited "Ole Miss"—only an hour's drive from his Memphis home —for the first time since he took the graphic photographs of the desegregation battles twenty-five years before.[4]

I came to know Mr. Withers first in my role as Director of the Afro-American Studies Program at the University of Mississippi from 1976 to 1982. In exploring the history of my native South, and especially the Civil Rights Movement which looms so large in this history, I found Mr. Withers' photographs at every turn. Over time, I gained a very dear friend whom I respect and admire because of the clarity and firmness of his views, the steadfastness of his convictions, and his sense of dedication to using his skills and tools in recording African-American history, and indeed, in shaping it.

Mr. Withers' documentation of the Civil Rights Era, and this exhibition and catalogue, are important in seeking to address the generation gap in conveying historical information about recent American history. Since the median age in the U.S. in 1989 was 32.7, this means that over half of the U.S. population was not born in 1958 when the momentous events covered in these civil rights photographs occurred. Thus, reiterating the facts and an interpretation of this pivotal period of U.S. history is an important educational and cultural contribution.[5] This is especially significant since we are approaching the 25th anniversary of Dr. King's death and the 1968 Memphis Sanitation Workers' strike. ⓰

[VIEWING BLACK HISTORY AND CIVIL RIGHTS: AN ANALYTICAL FRAMEWORK]

Photography, observed John Szarkowski, involves extensive "quot[ing] out of context."[6] What is the context which shaped Ernest Withers? How were his sensibilities as a photographer developed? What do his photographs seek to convey to us? To answer these questions, we must first develop a framework for assessing Black history and the Civil Rights Movement in the U.S.

FIGURE 16. *Sanitation Workers assemble in frnt of Clayborn Temple for a solidarity march. This was Dr. King's last march. Memphis, TN, March 28, 1968*

There are two important shortcomings in assessments of the Civil Rights Movement. First, the Civil Rights Movement is generally taken out of the context of Black history as a whole. People who make this mistake try to figure out "What do you people want?" by looking only at the period of the 1950s and 60s. Second, the Civil Rights Movement is usually cut off from the rich tradition of struggle which Black people have waged at various times for freedom, justice and equality.

These two pitfalls usually result in a failure to appreciate the deep historical roots of the Civil Rights Movement, its intensity, and how it and its partisans were linked to other social and political currents in Black history—Nationalism, Pan-Africanism, Socialism, Feminism, and Black Liberation Theology, among them.[7] The Civil Rights Movement was not a movement which just fell from the sky, and it is not a movement that will easily be swept off the stage of history or out of our historical consciousness, especially since so many of its issues are of present-day concern.

One corrective to this approach of isolating the Civil Rights Movement is to develop a framework which seeks to look inside the social reality of Black people—a reality which Ernest Withers knows all too well and sought to capture in his photographs. A careful assessment of this reality has led us to identify four central aspects of the Black experience.[8] First, the experiences of Black people have clearly been shaped by the factor of race, particularly color. Because people of African ancestry could generally be singled out, various social practices have operated which use color as a means of categorizing Black people for purposes of discrimination and other negative sanctions.

Second, people of African descent have always had very definite and distinct economic or class relationships within the United States. The slave trade and slavery contributed monumentally to the industrialization of Britain and the United States, just as sharecropping provided the cotton that was so essential to the development of the U.S. national economy after the end of slavery.[9] Class relations of Black people in the U.S. are still distinct, in degree if not in kind. In 1992, for example, poverty is more prevalent in the Black community than in any other, with 30.7% of Black people in poverty as compared with 10% for whites and 26.2% for Hispanics.

Third, there has evolved among Black people a definite nationality or foundation for a sense of peoplehood—distinct cultural practices, artistic expressions, and social institutions within Black communities throughout the U.S.

Finally, Black people, like others in this society, have formed complex belief systems that we call ideology, which shape their responses to all aspects of their social condition. For example, in response to racism as an ideology which seeks to rationalize the discriminatory treatment of Black people, Black people have embraced various liberation ideologies in the continuing struggle for freedom and justice.

These four components—race, class, nationality, and ideology—comprise the content which must be studied if we are to understand the Black experience.

But this content has not remained the same over historical time. The Black experience has been dynamically transformed through seven broad historical periods—Africa, the slave trade, slavery, Emancipation, rural life, migrations, and urban life. When the four aspects of Black life—race, class, nationality, and ideology—are combined on a four-by-seven diagram with the seven historical periods, we get a very useful framework to aid in the study of the Black Experience, one that is more comprehensive than many other approaches.[10]

In view of this approach, the Civil Rights Movement of which Mr. Withers was an integral part is really as old as this nation itself. In the slavery period, Black people were denied their recognition as human beings. "We hold these truths to be self-evident, that all men are created equal and endowed by their creator with certain unalienable rights," did not apply to slaves, nor even to white women. The Supreme Court made this clear in its decision in the Dred Scott case in 1854: "Black men have no rights that white men are bound to respect." All of this is ironic since until the 1840s, Africans constituted a majority of the people who migrated into the New World, and they made monumental contributions to the welfare of the new United States.

The Reconstruction Amendments effectively restored the human rights of slaves and established their civil rights—the 13th Amendment (1865) abolished slavery, the 14th Amendment (1868) extended equal protection of the laws, and the 15th Amendment (1870) granted the right to vote. From that point on, the basic political struggle of Black people was to have the U.S. government and the various states and local governments respect the civil rights that these laws represented. These laws were the basis for fighting the various disenfranchisement provisions (e.g., poll taxes, literacy clauses, grandfather clause) in the 19th century, and for battling these same provisions enforced by most southern states in the 20th century. The modern Civil Rights Movement—the subject of Mr. Withers' photographs—has its historical roots in these Reconstruction amendments.

The history of the 20th century Civil Rights Movement can best be understood as reflecting the evolution of various tactics in a struggle that was based on a strategic conception of reforming the political system of the U.S. These various tactics are amply illustrated in Mr. Withers' photographs. For example, the National Association for the Advancement of Colored People (NAACP), founded in 1909 and the Urban League, founded in 1914, were early proponents of the tactic of legal challenges. The Congress of Racial Equality or CORE (1945), the Southern Christian Leadership Council or SCLC (1956), and the Student Nonviolent Coordinating Committee, or SNCC (1966), were all champions of mass mobilization tactics. Given the strategic emphasis that all these organizations placed on winning the vote as the key to freedom, it should not be surprising that the third wave of organizations adopted electoral politics as the main tactic in the struggle for civil rights (e.g., Congressional Black Caucus).

This history is important for a proper introduction to this collection of photographs, which represent one man's perspective on the Civil Rights Movement. By understanding and valuing this perspective, we learn to value the role of Black people in articulating their relationship to the political order in the United States. This history also helps us understand what the Movement was about, and more importantly in this context, what historical dynamics spurred on women and men like Ernest Withers to put their lives on the line to realize the full measure of their history-making struggles.

From Ernest Withers and people like him, we see the Civil Rights Movement and Black history from the inside out, a vantage point too seldom granted African-Americans. The artist-photographer's image of Black people is a popular subject indeed, one that often yields unparalleled commercial success. "*I Dream a World*," the fine exhibit and catalogue of photographs of Black women, is one recent example, and the tremendous controversy surrounding the movie "*Mississippi Burning*" which depicted the Civil Rights Era, falls into this category.[11]

Important for us in this collection of Mr. Withers' photographs is the fact that those about whom history is written have often dared to tell their own story and the stories of their people. People like Ernest Withers lived and worked in places where intense struggles were being waged and battles won and lost. They were committed to preserving the truth through the camera's eye, or through

FIGURE 17. *Ernest Withers in front of Central High School, Little Rock, AR, 1957*

some other means. As Black photographers and journalists, they did not always enjoy the protection that their white counterparts experienced. This makes their commitment to fulfilling their mission something not to be taken lightly.

[A Biographical Sketch]

Ernest Withers [17] comes from solid African-American stock, with experiences more compelling than the subject matter of many movies. He was born in Memphis on August 7, 1922. His grandfather ran off to fight with the Union Army when it came through Mississippi, but returned home because of love for his family. He ignored warnings from other Black people to stay out of sight, and during a trip on which he chauffeured several white men, he disappeared. Pieces of his clothing were later found in a deserted area.

Ernest's father worked as a truck driver and as a driver for the U.S. Postal Service. "He was a strong family man," according to Mr. Withers, and active as a layman in the Baptist Church and with the local Black college. Ernest's mother, Pearl, died when he was eight. His stepmother, an expert seamstress, dressed the children in "beautiful little outfits… a better dress style than the average kid at that level…," recalls Withers. He also recounts a game they played in which his stepmother would cut pieces of cloth and send them to match threads at the local dry goods store. He attributes much of the patience it takes to be a photographer to this training:

"We got to be kind of keen in our patience, and I think this was the necessary patience I had to develop for life. It gave me an incentive for detail work in the graphic art of photography. It gave me an eye for selectivity, and it gave me patience in selecting… a tendency to pull things together… [This skill] was not really [the result of] a pattern of training, as I look back on it; it was an innate skill that had to be developed."

Mr. Withers attended Manassas High School in Memphis before serving in the U.S. Army between 1943 and 1946. He studied at the U.S. Army School of Photography and the Memphis Police Academy. He worked in various law enforcement agencies for Memphis and Tennessee. In 1942, he married his high school sweetheart, Dorothy Mae, and they raised eight children—seven sons and a daughter. Withers almost stumbled into his initial use of cameras; an older sister bought one as a birthday gift for a boyfriend who let young Ernest experiment with it at the age of twelve or thirteen. At one point, he took up a dare and broke all the rules for assemblies at

Manassas High—he walked to the front of school assembly to photograph Marva Trotter-Louis, the wife of the heavyweight champion, Joe Louis.

But his formal introduction to photography came later. A Black photographer in his Army unit, a Florida native, was slated for Army photography school at Fort Sutton, North Carolina. But when "the Florida boys got rowdy, an officer moved [the photographer] to be the platoon sergeant; and I was right at the spot, and made the request without any credentials" to be sent to photography school. And they did send him, in part because Withers had a respectful relationship to the company commander, a prominent white Tennessean.

Withers' instructor was "a German photographer...who gave me a good basic training, both lab and photographic practice. At that time, he made a suggestion that 'you ought to learn and learn well because it could be a future occupation.'" Even in this venue, discrimination reared its head.

"We would have to make the big marches. I was a private, and another guy would be a sergeant, and had more authority. He had his camera and I had mine, and he shot his pictures and I shot mine. He had less ability. He developed his pictures and I developed mine. Since mine were good, he wanted the [white] officer to take mine and make the presentation as his. We had a few problems with that. It just so happens that this guy and I had come along together in high school, and went in the Army together. Naturally, when you know a guy well, the level of resentment is greater."

Ernest Withers developed a well-honed consciousness of his place in Black intellectual history, playing a role not unlike the scholar W.E.B. DuBois, the writer Zora Neale Hurston, or several of the great Black journalists who preceded him. They used the pen and he used the camera. At the same time, he was well aware that he was helping to make and to shape history as he recorded and disseminated his images of struggle. His philosophy of photojournalism and social history was synthesized in an interview included in the brochure from our 1984 exhibition of his photographs at the University of Mississippi:

"Photography is a collection of memories. One who is trained in photography knows that. Instinctively, people who have an occupation know what they ought to do. You call the fireman to put out the fire; you call the police to solve a police problem; and people who are news people and journalists are collectors and recorders of present evidence... which after a given length of time—days, months, years— becomes history. The memories of yesterday—an old event—are continued and reflected upon.

Photography itself helps to teach what one should know. When I go through the negatives with various images out of the past, it has a tendency to jog my mind. The average person who doesn't go through such images doesn't have his or her mind refreshed about the past. It renews your memory. It starts you thinking retrospectively. But you can't get caught up in memories of the past. It has a tendency to give you the same mental tiredness as an accountant or bookkeeper who is looking at figures.

When I display a collection of images, people of today have certain feelings about the past, not just knowledge of history but a sense of knowing what has occurred. These images are just a recipe of the past. A woman who cooks in the kitchen might glance at certain recipes when she cooks another dish. I can look at pictures of persons looking at images. It's part of the visual culture and people are enriched through research. People go to the library for research on certain things. Ninety-five percent of the persons who go to the library for a specific thing come out of the library with a whole lot more than they went after because they are fed through their visual eye."

In the role as photographer-as-social activist, Ernest Withers would probably paraphrase a quote attributed to Karl Marx: "The point is not just to photograph the world, but to change it!" This could very well have been the Withers motto as he journeyed across the South covering the civil rights struggle:

"I have been covering the Civil Rights Era beginning in the 1950s through the death of Martin Luther King, Jr. and even as late as the 1970s. I have a running file on King's life and activity, but not only that, but on the activities and lives of other people that participated in the Civil Rights Movement. They moved from Montgomery, across the cotton fields of Mississippi to the Delta. In Mississippi, I covered the deaths of Lamar Smith of Hazelhurst, of the civil rights workers down in Neshoba County, and the death of Mack Parker in Poplarville. And the murder of Medgar Evers comes before that.

When James Meredith went to "Ole Miss," which I covered, there was a simultaneous rash of fires and gunfire at Black residences in the Lee County, Mississippi area. I did some door-to-door and house-to-house coverage on the rash of fires down there.

Before that, I did the Emmett Till case. I was at the Emmett Till trial from the beginning to the end. I have pictures of the press table, of the [Black] guy pointing to the [accused] murderer." Those pictures that *Black Star* distributed apparently they must have been gotten from the defendant. They didn't give me the credit but they were my shots, and I have the pictures in my file..."

Withers' account reveals just how much Black journalists were a part of making civil rights history, involved as active partisans in the struggle and not just as mere bystanders.

"Charles Wilson, who was the editor of the *Memphis Tri-State Defender*, covered the Till case. He went down and got "Too-Tight" Collins [who worked for one of Till's accused murderers], brought him out of Mississippi to Chicago, and they debriefed him up there. And then "Too-Tight" Collins came back to Mississippi and disappeared. It was said that they killed him... Simeon Booker and I went down to investigate what had happened to Collins. We found his father out on the farm, and we were talking with his father. I have this picture of his father's mule. Booker said he got more of the mule that he got of Too-Tight's father."

I should note here that Mr. Withers' accounts of his history include close relationships with several outstanding Black journalists and photojournalists who need to be studied in their own right, including Jimmy Hicks of the *Amsterdam News*, L. Alex Wilson and L.O. Swingler of the *Memphis Tri-State Defender*, Tresvan Anderson of the *Pittsburgh Courier*, Nat Williams of the *Memphis World*, Ted Polston of the *New York Post*, Moses Newsome of the *Baltimore Afro-American*, Howard Woods of the *St. Louis Sentinel*, Mrs. Tanner Mitchell of the *St. Louis Argus*; Simeon Booker, Larry Still, Maurice Sorrell and Moneta Sleet, all of *Jet*, and Clotilde Murdock of *Ebony*.[12]

There was considerable danger in being a Black photographer or journalist covering the Civil Rights Movement in the deep South, a fact underscored by the murder of a French journalist during the turmoil which accompanied the desegregation struggle at "Ole Miss." Withers has his share of war stories. In Little Rock, Withers describes how white women protesting the integration of schools spat in his face. In Belzoni, Mississippi, Withers and his compatriots had only a few minutes to do a story on Gus Coates who was shot in his grocery store. "We took so many pictures so quick and so fast the woman said 'Y'all ain't from Memphis; y'all from that Colored paper in Chicago.' Twenty minutes later we were back in the car and gone before she had gone down and told her boss that there were some people down there from Chicago takin' pictures where Mr. Lee was shot. So we were out and gone."

His experience while photographing the funeral of Medgar Evers in 1963 illustrates the personal danger he faced.

"A white man with a long knife tried to break through the line to get at the crowd of marchers, but he was stopped and roughed up by officers... Then officers started grabbing demonstrators who were in the streets and began beating and kicking them as they pushed them toward the trucks. Women, men and teenagers were being beaten and all of the time I was standing on the sidewalk taking one horrible scene after the other amid the screams. Suddenly a burly white man who was not an officer, but looked more like one of the sanitation employees, came over and snatched me into the street. The force of the movement took the top off of my camera. As I tried to retrieve it, a policeman came over and began beating me with a nightstick and ushering me toward the truck."

On other occasions, fear almost overwhelmed him. Withers describes one particular visit to Poplarville, Mississippi where the sight of Black men on the streets during the week raised questions.

Medgar Evers lies in state at the Mason's Temple. Daisy Bates looks on. Jackson, MS, 1963

"My writer Simeon Booker said 'When we get there, you say you're from the South. You just tell these folks where you're from, and you answer most of the questions until we get ourselves in.' And so the man said, 'Where y'all from?' I opened my mouth about five times, and nothing came out. It was just that much fear in me... I didn't realize I was that frightened. And Booker said, 'I'm from Maryland.' And, of course, after he talked about three minutes maybe, I loosened up to talk."

When Withers provides even a partial list of the civil rights struggles he photographed, his fear is understandable: in Mississippi, the murder trial of Emmett Till, Philadelphia and Neshoba County after the murder of Chaney, Schwerner, and Goodman; the tour to test the desegregation of public accommodations, and the Medgar Evers funeral; in Alabama, the Montgomery Bus Boycott; in Arkansas, the desegregation of Central High in Little Rock; in Tennessee, the Tent City protest in Fayette County, the years of struggle in Memphis, the Sanitation Workers' strike and the assassination of Dr. King, and many other battles.

Ernest Withers is important too because he took such great care to spread the word about his work, and even more important because of what his photographs represent in recording Black history. One example of this is his book, *Reflections in History: Pictures Tell the Story*, ambitiously labeled "*Volume 1*" when it was published in 1984. Asked why he started the publication, he responded: "It was an opportunity to reflect our past. We must have that same reflective feeling that one would have if one was looking down into a reflecting pool, or looking into a mirror. We have had such a [intense] collection of energies which have come out of the past."

A more potent example, however, is the "*Complete Photo Story of Till Murder Case*" which we have included in this catalogue. There can be no bolder testimony to his commitment to making sure that the real story of why Mississippi was burning was known, and who was struggling to put out the fire.[13]

On the last page of "*Reflections in History*" there is a long poem "*I am Photography*." I am certain it was selected for inclusion because it provides us with some insight into how Withers views his craft:

"I carry the news of the world, and bring you visions of far Distant Lands. Though men may die and empires may crumble in the dust, my magic will preserve their likeness for future generations... I illumine the pages of history, and make learning possible for the multitude..."

This learning "for the multitude" is especially focused on the importance of history. "One has a greater appreciation for the present," he told me, "when you have a memory of the past." Withers sees his photographs as representing an essential element of continuity from one generation to the next.

I have made no effort in this essay to develop a detailed interpretation of the individual civil rights photographs in this selection. This is an important task which remains to be done. I am constantly struck, however, by a distinct angle of vision which Withers repeatedly brings to his work. As I said earlier, it is his perch from inside the Black experience which lends power and credibility to his photographs. One outstanding example is a key photograph in this exhibit: the picture of a bumper sticker on the back of a shiny new Pontiac in downtown Memphis in 1952: "*Don't Buy Gas Where You Can't Use the Rest Room,*" it admonishes. It heralds part of the untold story.

The sticker includes the name of the sponsoring organization, the Regional Council of Negro Leadership. This organization was headed by Dr. T.R.M. Howard, a doctor in Mound Bayou, Mississippi. Dr. Howard was founder of the Magnolia Mutual Insurance Company and hoped that the Council would

FIGURE 19

be spared the harassment faced by the NAACP. Dr. Howard was a mentor for numerous young Black leaders in the region; Medgar Evers joined the insurance company as an agent upon his graduation from college in 1952.[14]

There are other examples. *Powerful Days: The Civil Rights Photography of Charles Moore* contains excellent photographs from the battle to desegregate the University of Mississippi. But Mr. Withers' photograph of the Black journalist Jimmy Hicks in the press room of the still-segregated administration building says much about an aspect of the struggle he saw as important. And more compelling is Mr. Withers' photo of the white FBI agents in the basement of the same building with the many guns and other weapons confiscated from rioters at the University of Mississippi . This photo tellingly underscores the serious meaning of a sign carried by a protestor in another one of his photographs: "*Segregation or War!*"

Perhaps most important about Mr. Withers' photographs is their obvious testimony that the masses of people are the makers of history. There are numerous pictures of leaders: Rosa Parks, Martin Luther King, Fannie Lou Hamer, Bayard Rustin, Stokely Carmichael, Whitney Young, Ralph Abernathy, Andrew Young, Floyd McKissick, Bernard Lee and many others. Photographs of Memphis leaders include Attorney A.W. Willis, Reverend Benjamin Hooks, Maxine Smith, Attorney Russell Sugarmon and T.O. Jones.

But there is also a sea of unnamed Black faces in many of Withers' photographs. Though we will never know all of their names, we do know the effectiveness of the movement which they mounted, and his photographs are graphic testimony that they were there —by the tens, by the hundreds, and by the thousands.

A project such as this always raises justifiable concern about the depiction of the role of women and particularly the role of Black women. The title of one of the classic texts in Black women's studies captured the essence of how the contributions of Black women have been distorted: *All the Women are White, All the Blacks are Men, But Some of Us Are Brave* (edited by Hull, Scott, and Smith and published by Feminist Press in 1982). We share this concern.

Women played an absolutely vital role in the Civil Rights Movement. This should not surprise us, for it was a continuation of their leadership role in all historical periods of the Black experience—from Queen Nzinga's fight against Portuguese colonial encroachment in the 1600s, to the anti-slavery work of women like Harriet

Tubman and Sojourner Truth, the anti-lynching battles of Ida B. Wells, the educational work of Mary McLeod Bethune, the civil rights organizing of Ella Baker and Fannie Lou Hamer, and the union organizing and internationalist work of such women as Vicki Garvin of New York City. The list could go on and on!

But we cannot re-photograph the images of Ernest Withers as we come to better understand the male biases in our presentation of history, nor should we want to. And we do not have to! Ernest Withers' photographs amply convey the centrality of the role of women in the Civil Rights Movement. We see leaders such as Rosa Parks of Montgomery, Fannie Lou Hamer in Mississippi, Daisy Bates in Little Rock, Attorney Constance Baker Motley of the NAACP Legal Defense Fund, and Maxine Smith in Memphis. Even six of the Little Rock Nine were girls!

But we also see women prominent among the masses of people in the Movement: carrying signs; directing marches; traveling to the Poor People's Campaign, and in all other roles. Even the poignant photos of Myrlie Evers and Coretta King with their families after their husbands were murdered reminds us of this important and often unheralded contribution that women were too often called upon to make.

Julie Ann Briscoe, Memphis NAACP, protests on Main Street. Memphis, TN, early 1960s

But it remains the case that the role of women is all too often invisible in the historical record. The Montgomery Bus Boycott is but one example. While we all know the role played by Dr. King, fewer people might recall the contribution of Mrs. Parks. But hardly anyone can discuss the role of the Women's Political Council, headed by Professor JoAnn Robinson of the English Department at Alabama State University. Her organization wrote to Montgomery's mayor in May 1954—a year before the bus boycott catapulted Dr. King to international prominence.

She demanded "a city law that would make it possible for Negroes to sit from back toward front, and whites from front toward back until all the seats are taken...Three fourths of the riders... are Negroes, if Negroes did not ride them they could not possibly operate," and she mentioned that "There has been talk from twenty-five or more local organizations of planning a city-wide boycott of busses." Mrs. Robinson's book is superbly titled: *The Montgomery Bus Boycott and the Women who Started It* (University of Tennessee, 1987).

In sum, the title of my friend Charles Payne's essay on women in the Mississippi movement is an excellent reiteration of a point which needs more emphasis: "*Men Led, But Women Organized!*" [15]

Finally, the life and work of Mr. Withers brings to the fore a certain set of values which must have operated for him and many of his contemporaries. He does not have the fame nor the fortune of Gordon Parks, a Black photographer who was a member of the FSA photographic team, for example. But Withers is clear on his motivations. "My feelings of self-worth are intact because I know that I was able to serve people by doing something I loved and because of this talent, I was able to make a contribution." [16]

And despite the fact that he has taken thousands of photographs of events which often reflect the tremendous racial polarization in the U.S., Mr. Withers is very clear that his photographs should contribute to ending racial polarization. "If a guy has a good taste about life, he can look back on the past without having any poor taste or feelings. So I don't think that images out of the past polarize [us]." His photographs, by addressing an important yet painful period of our national history, seek to restore some of the "good taste" about this aspect of our lives.

For all of these reasons, the photographs of Ernest Withers represent a veritable gold mine of possibilities as we approach the 21st century, perhaps no closer to solving the perplexing racial crisis facing this nation than when Dr. W.E.B. DuBois wrote perceptively in *The Souls of Black Folk* (1903), "the problem of the 20th century is the problem of the color line."

[Conclusion]

The past several years have been a special time in the history of the Civil Rights Movement. Because many of these events occurred in the 1960s, this has been a period of 25th and 30th anniversary commemorations. More recently, the policies of the Bush administration, the resignation of Justice Thurgood Marshall from the U.S. Supreme Court and the appointment of Judge Clarence Thomas have resulted in intensifying debate about civil rights and affirmative action.

Given that we are still addressing such fundamental questions as equal rights for all U.S. citizens more than 200 years after this nation's founding, it is imperative that we escalate our effort to see, in the words of U.N. diplomat Ralph Bunche (who appears in a Withers photograph at the funeral of Medgar Evers) why this nation has failed to "democ" for so many of its people, especially Black people and people of color. [20]

I must express my deepest concern regarding the course of current discussions regarding the place of African-American history in the curriculum and in our national consciousness, often couched in discussions about multicultural education and cultural diversity. As a humanities scholar, all of this presents a special challenge to me. Though the humanities are often thought of in terms of disciplines, the more challenging definitions are those which seek to convey a sense of what should result from studying or being exposed to humanities scholarship: "habits of mind," as they are termed in a recent report from the National Center for History in the Schools. These include, for example, "a tolerance for the complexity of human affairs" and "history empathy," or the ability to view events through the eyes of those living at the time."

Nowhere is this mandate more pressing than in race relations in the U.S. It is my firm belief that the photography of Ernest Withers, the scholarship over the past few years and related projects can have a positive impact if we approach the subject intelligently.

Too often the discussion is viewed as a zero-sum game—if Black history is discussed, then the history of whites must be negated. If certain ethnic groups are included, then other ethnic groups must be excluded. My firm view is that it is possible, indeed necessary, to conduct a discussion of Black history, and specifically the history of the Civil Rights Movement in the U.S., where the vast majority of all people are winners. Rather than bashing each other, it is past time that we took seriously our collective responsibility for a challenge not yet realized in the slogan "*E Pluribus Unum,*" and echoed poetically by the Afro-American poet laureate Langston Hughes: "Let America be America again, the land that never has been yet, and yet must be. America has never been America to me. And yet, I swear this oath, America will be!"

The photographs of Ernest C. Withers —and this exhibition and catalogue— are steps in the direction of educating the next generation, and of revitalizing the memories and political motion of this generation as well. Mr. Withers is clear on this role of his photographs in recording history and in motivating us to take history into our own hands and to help make it. These photographs and the future of Black people and of this society are full of what the Civil Rights Movement and all of Black history have been about—the imperative to create a more just and humane society.

We join with the millions of voices who on countless occasions over the past have sung the words of "Lift Every Voice and Sing," the National Negro Anthem, and we say as loudly and boldly as the photographs of Ernest Withers do: "LET US MARCH ON!"

Ronald W. Bailey
Chairperson
Department of African-American Studies
Northeastern University

---

1. *Dr. Maryemma Graham provided detailed comments on an earlier draft of this essay which dramatically improved its clarity; and she has shared my enthusiasm for honoring the work of Mr. Withers. Rosemary Williams, my current administrative assistant and a friend of Mr. Withers, has worked above and beyond the call of duty to bring this project to a successful completion. Charlotte Gator and Marilyn Houston, secretary and research assistant at the University of Mississippi, worked on the first Withers exhibit. Dr. Barbara Hunt and Dr. E. Patricia Murrain, research associates at the University of Mississippi, also contributed to this overall effort.*

2. *For coverage of the 150th anniversary of photography, see, for example, "Photography: The Camera has a Happy 150th Birthday," **Time** (February 27, 1989) and "150 Years of Photography," **Maclean's** (April 24, 1989).*

3. *Information about this conference can be obtained from the Center for the Study of Southern Culture, Dr. William Ferris, Director and Dr. Ann Abadie, Associate Director. An award-winning video documentary was also produced: "Dateline Freedom: Civil Rights and the Press" by WETA, Washington. The description of the video in the PBS catalogue reiterates my point about the shortcomings in our understanding of the role Black journalists played during this period: "Mostly white, mostly male, and mostly Southern, these journalists shared their recollections at a reunion in Oxford, Mississippi, where* *they discuss their participation in one of the most important movements in recent history."*

4. *It should not have surprised me that many Black people in Mississippi had such little contact with "Ole Miss." For example, a leading social scientist at Alcorn reported at one of the annual conferences on Black Mississippians I organized, that she grew up in the shadow of the campus but had not visited it until she joined us in 1980. On another occasion, we hosted Dr. Margaret Walker, the noted writer, and delegates during the Mississippi* NAACP *state conference in Oxford. It was the first time that civil rights stalwarts such as Mr. C.C. Bryant of McComb and many others had ever visited the campus. The story can be repeated many times. The University has sought to address this issue by presenting annually a series of awards to prominent Black Mississippians.*

5. *For an example of what young people can do with the history of the Civil Rights Movement, both as consumers and as producers of knowledge, see the work of my friend at* ROCC *in Holmes County, Mississippi:* Youth of the Rural Organizing Culture Center, Holmes County, MS. **Minds Stayed on Freedom: The Civil Rights Struggle in the Rural South** *(Westview, 1991).*

6. *Cited in Nicholas Nathanson,* **The Black Image in the New Deal: The Politics of FSA Photography**, *(University of Tennessee Press, 1992), p. 10.*

7. *Abdul Alkalimat has usefully reviewed these ideological and political trends as mainstays of the 20th century Black liberation movement in his* **Studies on Malcolm X: A Review Essay and Research Design**, *Sage Race Relations Abstracts (Fall 1992).*

8. *The framework I am summarizing can be found in more detail in a textbook I co-authored, Alkalimat and Associates,* **Introduction to Afro-American Studies: A Peoples College Primer** *(1982).*

9. *See, for example, Ronald W. Bailey, "The Slave(ry) Trade and the Development of Capitalism in the United States: The Textile Industry in New England," in Inikori and Engermann,* **The Atlantic Slave Trade** *(Duke, 1992). The extensive writings of Douglas C. North contain additional discussion.*

10. *For an application of this framework to Mississippi, including a discussion of civil rights and more recent developments, see Ronald W. Bailey, "Black/White Relations in Mississippi," Chapter 7 in Boucher, Landis, and Arnold (eds.),* **Ethnic Conflict: Myth and Reality in the 1980s** *(Beverly Hills: Sage Publications, 1987).*

11. *"I Dream A World" consisted of photographs by Brian Lanker and was published in 1989 by Stewart, Tabori, and Chang. For a glimpse of the "Mississippi Burning" controversy, see the following articles in* **The New York Times**: *"Vietnam Behind It, Hollywood Turns to the Civil Rights Struggle" (April 19, 1988); "Civil Rights, Burned" (December 30, 1988, editorial); "Retracing Mississippi's Agony" (December 9 and December 18, 1988; comment and review by Vincent Canby); and "Fact vs. Fiction in Mississippi" (December 4, 1988, by Wayne King).*

12. *Henry. G. LaBrie, III (ed.),* **Perspective on the Black Press** *(Mercer House Press, 1973) is one starting point for the history of the Black press.*

13. *"Why Was Mississippi Burning and Who Put Out the Fire" was a 1989 symposium I organized in Jackson, Mississippi to discuss the distortion of civil rights history in the film. We brought together an impressive number of leading activists from the 1960s to discuss the film, and more importantly, to discuss other ways to tell the untold story of the Movement. Videotapes from this conference will soon be available.*

14. *A rare photograph of Dr. Howard with Medgar Evers was supplied by Myrlie Evers and is included in* **Remembering Medgar Evers... for a New Generation**. *Taylor Branch,* Parting the Waters *discusses the comments Dr. Howard made at Medgar Evers' funeral in which he described the sticker campaign.*

15. *This article appears in one of the most valuable contributions to this discussion to appear in the last few years,* **Women in the Civil Rights Movement: Trailblazers and Torchbearers, 1941-1965**, *edited by Crawford, Rouse, Woods, Butler, Dryden and Walker (Carlson, 1990). The book was developed from a conference held in Atlanta in 1987.*

16. *Quoted in the* **Memphis Commercial Appeal**, *February 20, 1990, p. c1.*

20. *Ralph Bunche's research memorandum for Gunnar Myrdal's* **American Dilemma** *remains one of the classic discussions of the Black political experience during the rural period. See Bunche,* **The Political Status of the Negro in the Age of F.D.R.**

The Emmett Till Murder Trial
Sumner, MS, 1955

Mississippi was the leading cotton-producing state in the U.S. in 1860, and hence had the largest slave population concentrated especially in the Delta region along the Mississippi River. It was a majority Black state from 1840 to 1940—a full century! After slavery, there was a brief participation of Black people in electoral politics—two Black U.S. senators were elected—and then a return to almost complete disenfranchisement and racist violence. Despite a Black-majority population, no Black person was elected to the U.S. Congress between the 1880s and 1984, when Congressman Mike Espy was elected. Economic deprivation was as intense, and Mississippi has had one of the highest poverty rates of any state in the U.S.

This history laid the basis for the explosion of civil rights activity in the 1960s. But the struggle did not begin then. In 1952, for example, Dr. T.R.M. Howard, a Mound Bayou physician and businessman, led a statewide campaign to put some 40,000 fluorescent bumper stickers on cars saying *"Don't Buy Gas Where You Can't Use the Rest Room."*

In 1955, Emmett Till, a 14 year-old from Chicago who had just graduated from grammar school, journeyed to Mississippi to visit his grandparents, uncles, aunts, and cousins—a pilgrimage of many Black people in Chicago. The story of his ghastly killing is graphically chronicled in a pamphlet produced by Mr. Withers in 1955. Young Till was dragged from his house and brutally beaten and murdered by two white men, relatives of a white woman to whom Till was alleged to have said "Bye, baby"—a violation of Southern racial codes. Despite a nationally publicized trial in Sumner, Mississippi—with startling testimony by Emmett's uncle Mose Wright and with U.S. Congressman Diggs of Michigan in attendance—both men were declared innocent. Later, they confessed the murder to William Bradford Huie, who paid them for their testimony for a story he published in *Look*.

Murders of Black people were not new to Mississippi, especially after the 1954 U.S. Supreme Court decision outlawing desegregation. But the Emmett Till murder had a profound impact. The dramatic pictures of the beaten and bloated body in *Jet* and other coverage increased the anger of Black people after the murderers were found innocent, and then confessed. The Till murder was the catalyst needed to escalate the Civil Rights Movement in the South and in the nation.

Well-known Mississippi activist Amzie Moore stated "they had newspapers from all over the continent of North America, some from India, and it was the best advertised lynching that I had ever heard. Personally, I think this was the beginning of the Civil Rights Movement in Mississippi in the twentieth century. From that point on, Mississippi began to move." And so did others: it is no accident that Rosa Parks sparked the Montgomery Bus Boycott only a few months after Emmett Till's brutal murder. Throughout the South, a generation of returning World War II and Korean War veterans who had fought to make the world safe for democracy vowed to make U.S. democracy safe for Black people at home.

RWB

Emmett Till

26

COMPLETE PHOTO STORY OF TILL MURDER CASE

FIRST AND ONLY COMPLETE, FACTUAL PHOTO STORY OF TILL CASE

Send Check or Money Order With Your Name and Address Payable To

WITHER'S PHOTOGRAPHERS
P. O. Box 2505
Memphis, Tenn.

AUTHENTIC PICTURES TAKEN ON THE SPOT DESIGNED TO MEET PUBLIC DEMAND

price: $1.00
Per Booklet

THE STORY BEGINS when handsome, 14-year old Emmett Till of Chicago (see cover), who when younger had been a victim of polio, but who now was a strapling lad whose only souvenir of his bout with polio was the sometimes habit of stuttering, was granted permission to visit his uncle Mose Wright (last right, seen with his son Robert, 14), 64 year old cotton farmer in the small (350 population Magnolia state cotton center of Money, Miss. (left.).

The visiting youth's vacation moved along nicely until Aug. 28, the fifth day of his visit, when he, in the company of several other youths, visited Bryant's Grocery (center) in Money and started a chain of events that was later to focus the eyes of the nation and the world upon Mississippi . . .

PREFACE

The question naturally arises, why such a pamphlet as this? "Crass Commercialism", one cynic might snort or another label it as "Outright Exploitation", but neither of these would be true.

This pamphlet was designed first as the most expedient method to meet the demands for pictures of the Till trial. Well aware that the supplying of the pictures on an individual basis would prove time consuming and financially exorbitant, the originator felt that the most effective way to meet the demand was to group the pictures into a factual, objective pictorial story painting.

Secondly, as the booklet began to take shape, we felt that this booklet could also contribute to the Sociological Field of Race Relations.

For in presenting this photo story on the Emmett Till Murder Trial, we are not only depicting the plight of an individual Negro, but rather of life as it affects all Negroes in the United States.

Even tho the incidents depicted happened in Mississippi, a state where Negroes comprise slightly less than one half of the population (2,178,914 according to the 1950 census), but less than 20,000 are registered voters, a state which from 1882 to 1953 was the scene of 574 lynch killings, a state where a Negro minister, the Rev. George W. Lee of Belzoni, was slain for allegedly refusing to take his name off the registration list, a state where another Negro, Lamar Smith, was slain openly in the Brookhaven Courthouse Square for his alleged political activities—this booklet is not only about Mississippi but shows what has happened in that state and can happen in other states.

In brief we are presenting this photo story not in an attempt to stir up racial animosities or to question the verdict in the Till Murder Case, but in the hope that this booklet might serve to help our nation dedicate itself to seeing that such incidents need not occur again.

To this End we dedicate this pamphlet!

P.S.—This pamphlet is an individual project and is not sponsored by any organization or any type!

. . . Ernest C. Withers, Photographer

Entire Contents Copyright
1955 by Ernest Withers
Photographer

WHILE IN THE STORE the visiting Chicago lad alledgedly "wolf whistled" at the storekeeper's pretty wife, Mrs. Carolyn Bryant, 21 (insert.) Testifying later in court Mrs. Bryant said the youth asked "how about a date?" and attempted to put his arms around her waist.

Later that night Mrs. Bryant's husband, Roy, 24 (right), accompanied by his half brother J. W. Milam, 36 of Glendora, Miss. (left,) went out to Mr. Wright's home.

ARRIVING AT MR. WRIGHT'S house (left) the two men demanded to see "that boy that did that talking up in Money!" They took the visiting Negro lad from his bed (right) and departed to find out "if he was the right boy." The Till lad was not seen alive after that.

The two men claimed they turned the youth loose after they learned he wasn't the right boy, but later a badly battered, decomposed body turned up in the Tallahatchie river and was identified as the Till youth mainly on the strength of a ring bearing the initials "L. T." identified as having been given to the Chicago lad by his late father Louis Till.

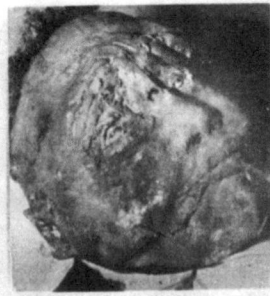

FOLLOWING THE DISCOVERY of the body the scene shifted to Chicago, Ill., where for three days some 50,000 persons viewed the youth's mutilated body (right) At the funeral services the youth's mother, Mrs. Mamie Bradley (left), distressingly cried" I hope my son did not die in vain."

The scene then shifted back to Mississippi where the state, heeding the demands of an aroused nation, sought to have the two white half brothers tried. First on the murder charge, later on the kidnap charge.

SUMNER, MISSISSIPPI, a farming town of about 780 population, whose motto, ironic enough, is "A Good Place To Raise A Boy," was chosen as the site for the murder trial since the body was found in Tallahatchie County of which Sumner is the county seat.

SUMNER'S HISTORIC COURTHOUSE was focused into the world's spotlight as an influx of approximately 70 Negro and white representatives of national and international mediums of mass communications and hundreds of other curious persons taxed the 138 capacity courthouse to hear the hectic five day trial.

TRIAL JUDGE for the Bryant-Milam Till murder case was Circuit Court Judge Curtis M. Swango, described as one of Mississippi's most able jurors. Trial observers lauded the fair, impartial manner in which Judge Swango conducted the trial.

At right are the five defense attorneys who defended the half brothers: Harvey Henderson, J. W. Kellum, John W. Whitten Jr., J. J. Breland and C. Sidney Carlton.

PROSECUTING FOR THE STATE were Dist. Atty. Gerald Gerald Chatham of Hernando, Robert B. Smith III, a special assistant attorney general and Hamilton Caldwell, Tallahatchie County prosecuting attorney.

Emmett Till

29

DEFENDANTS IN THE MURDER case were Roy Bryant, 24, of Money, and his half brother J. W. Milam, 36, of Glendora. The two men were accompanied thruout the trial by their two sons, their wives and Bryant's mother.

MRS. MAMIE BRADLEY, mother of the slain youth, created a stir on the second day of the trial, when she arrived in Sumner from Chicago accompanied (left) by Rayfield Moody of Chicago, a relative by marriage and (right) her father John L. Cathran of Detroit.

SHERIFF H. C. STRIDER (right), a hefty 270 pounder, served Mrs. Bradley with a subpoena to serve as a state witness. Mrs. Bradley's testimony was used to aid the state in establishing the identity of the body as her son. During a court recess Mrs. Bradley met Dr. A. H. McCoy (left), outspoken Jackson, Miss., dentist and state NAACP president. For his NAACP activities in the state Dr. McCoy's life has been reportedly repeatedly threatened. Another key Mississippi NAACP officer attending the trial was Medgar Evers, state field director.

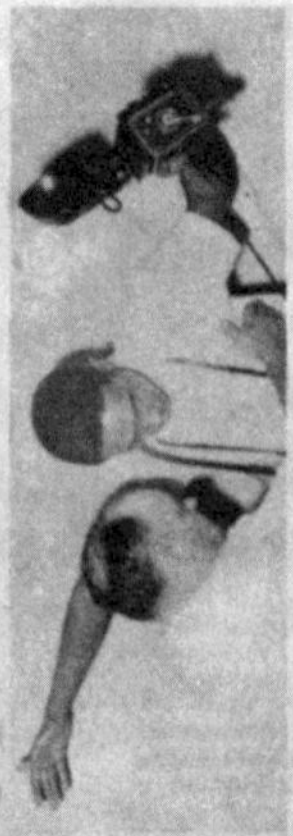

ALLEGEDLY HAVING RECEIVED numerous threats Sheriff Strider ordered his deputies to frisk all spectators and newsmen entering (for concealed weapons). Here (above) Deputy Shelby frisks St. Louis Argus photographer William B. Franklin. Congressman Charles C. Diggs, Jr. (below, center), Michigan's first Negro representative, added to the Till murder case drama when he arrived during the second day of the trial to sit in as an "interested observer." Cong. Diggs was accompanied by two Detroit lawyers Basil Brown (left) and James Del Rio (right).

FIRST WITNESS for the state was Mose Wright (standing), the slain youth's uncle shown here with Mrs. Bradley and her father during a court recess. Highpoint of Mr. Wright's testimony occured when he dramatically pointed to the two white half brothers as the men who entered his home and carried young Till away.

At right Dr. T. R. M. Howard, militant Mound Bayou physician (left) and Mrs. Ruby Hurley (right of Birmingham, southeastern NAACP director, accompany surprise witness Walter Billups into the courtroom. Dr. Howard was instrumental in turning up the surprise witnesses who attempted to establish the place where the killing took place.

SURPRISE WITNESSES FOR the state, seen here with Mr. Wright, Mrs. Bradley and her father, included Amanda Bradley (no relation to Mrs. Bradley), Walter Reed and Walter Billups, all of whom live on or near the Milam farm and who reported hearing noises in the Milam barn which sounded as if someone was being beaten.

KEY STATE AND DEFENSE witnesses were (left) Chester A. Miller, Greenwood undertaker to whose establishment the Till body was first carried, who testified for the State in an attempt to establish positive identification of the body and (right) Dr. L. B. Otkins, who examined the body, was a witness for the defense contending that the body was so badly decomposed he couldn't tell whether it was white or negro.

FOLLOWING all testimony by state and defense witnesses and summary arguments by defense and state counsels, as the jury retired to the jury room on the fifth and final day of the trial, a tense group of Negro spectators in their specially reserved section await the verdict of the jury.

Emmett Till

31

AN HOUR AND SEVEN MINUTES after this male, all white jury had retired to the juryroom they returned to announce that they had reached a verdict. Jury foreman J. A. Shaw (third from right, front row) announced that "We the jurors find the defendants not guilty."

Negro spectators reacted with shocked disbelief and one woman was heard to murmur "Oh, no!"

Members of the jury were Jim Pennington, Gus Ramsey, Ed Devaney, L. L. Price, Bishop Matthews, Howard Armstrong, Shaw, Ray Tribble, James Toole, George Holland, and Travis Thomas.

CLEARED OF THE MURDER charge the two half brothers, Roy Bryant and J. W. Milam, leave court carrying their two sons. Tho cleared on the murder of the visiting Negro youth the two men are expected to face trial in another county on the kidnap charges.

THE FINALE TO THE Bryant-Milam case has not yet been written as Leflore County Sheriff George W. Smith in whose county the kidnapping occurred announced that he will ask the grand jury to indict the two men on the kidnap charge.

School Desegregation
Little Rock, AR, 1957

In 1954, the U.S. Supreme Court effectively reversed the Plessy v. Ferguson ruling of 1896, which had declared that segregation was legal under the rubric of "separate but equal."

The Court now ruled "that in the field of public education the doctrine of 'separate but equal' has no place. Separate educational facilities are inherently unequal." The response across the South was intense and often furious.

The state of Arkansas shared many of the characteristics of Mississippi and other states in the Deep South. In 1940, about 25% of its population was Black, and 78% lived in rural areas. Little Rock, Arkansas' capital and only large city, had a sizeable Black population, and it is no surprise that it became the center of civil rights activity in the state.

On September 4, 1957, Governor Orville Faubus ordered the National Guard to the all-white Central High School to prevent the enrollment of a group of Black students, who came to be known as "The Little Rock Nine." It was a bold challenge that counterposed the armed might of state government in opposition to federal authority. After days of procrastination, President Eisenhower finally ordered 1000 soldiers from the 101st Airborne to Little Rock to protect the nine students and to bolster the authority of the U.S. government.

There were remarkable people involved in the Little Rock crisis. Most important were the nine students: Minnie Jean Brown, Elizabeth Eckford, Ernest Green, Thelma Mothershed, Gloria Ray, Melba Pattillo, Terrance Roberts, Jefferson Thomas, and Carlotta Walls. The story of Ms. Daisy Bates, advisor to the Little Rock Nine, is an important reminder of the leading role played by Black women in key struggles in the Civil Rights Movement. It is also the story of the role of key social institutions in the Black community: Ms. Bates was editor of the Arkansas State Press and president of the Arkansas NAACP.

Little Rock continues to play itself out. Arkansas native and Democratic presidential hopeful Bill Clinton should be elected as this book is coming off the press, if the polls are accurate. He has spoken eloquently and convincingly of the impact of the struggle for racial justice on his own political development. And Ernie Green, the only Senior among the Little Rock Nine and the sole Black student who graduated with his class in 1958, is one of Bill Clinton's close advisors and friends.

RWB

Desegregation of Central High School by "Little Rock Nine." (l to r) Carlotta Walls, Melba Patillo, Elizabeth Eckford and Minnie Jean Brown. Little Rock, AR, 1957

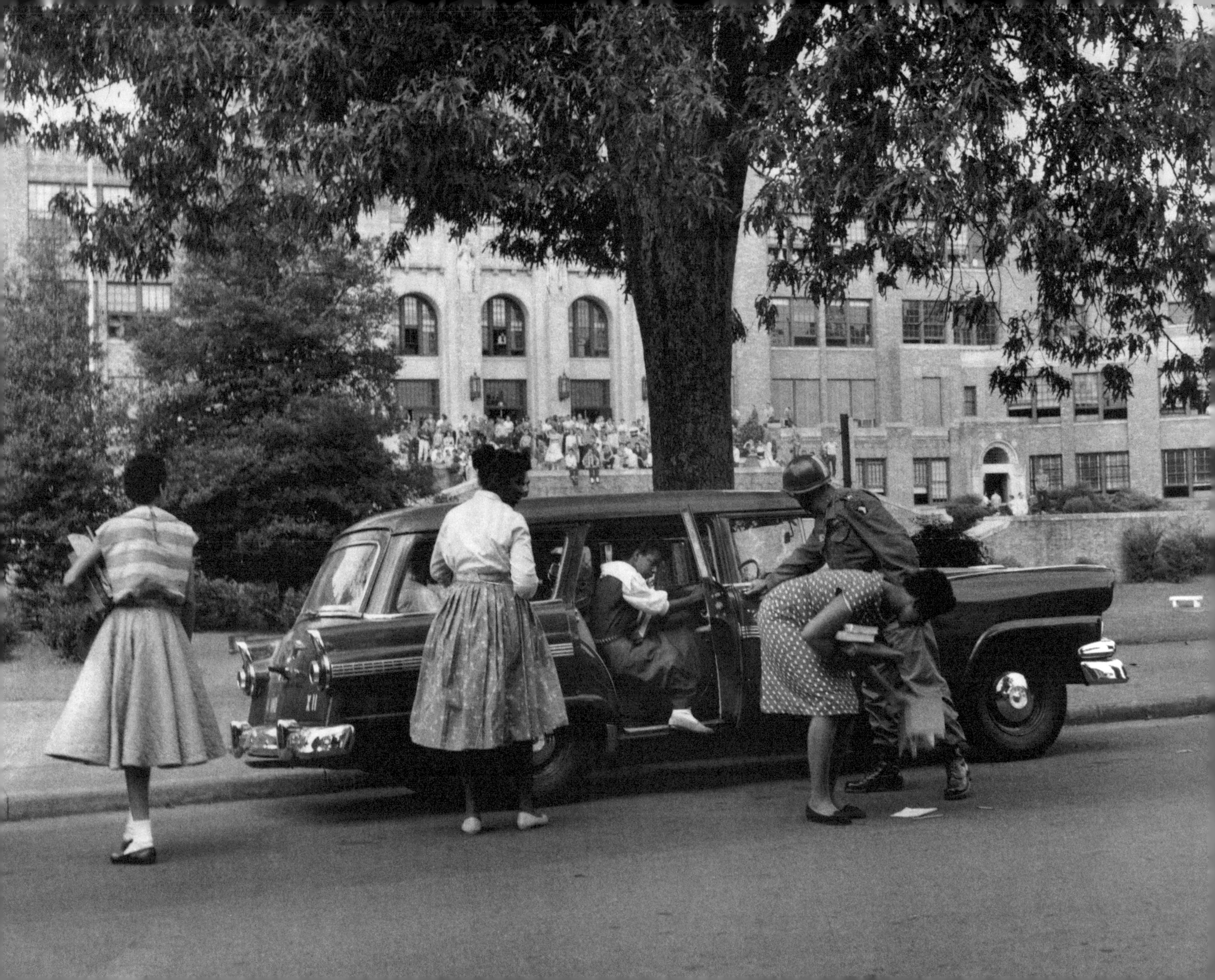

National Guard blocking integration of Central High School, Little Rock AR, 1957

Memphis, Tennessee
in the 1950s and 1960s

Memphis, Tennessee is named after the city of Memphis, an ancient city of Egypt, about fifteen miles south of Cairo. The name in Egyptian means "place of good abode," a reference that was often used in the Tennessee city's promotional literature. Memphis has long been the center of the mid-South, a veritable crossroads of transportation and commerce. For some years after 1892, most trains crossed here and five of seven national highways used the Hanrahan Bridge at Memphis, the only crossing between Cape Girardeau, Missouri and Louisiana. It is not surprising that in the 1940s, Memphis accounted for about 33% of all the cotton sales in the U.S.

The reality of segregation, necessary to maintain political and economic control of a large Black population, was as real in Memphis as in any Southern city. There were segregated waiting rooms and restrooms in train and bus stations and in all public facilities. And there was even a day when only Black people could go to the Memphis Zoo! Some would say that it was a sign of progress that Blacks could go at all!

Beyond the reputation of "Beale Street, Where the Blues Were Born," there was a sizeable Black Memphis community, with significant leadership and financial resources which could be mustered to fight the old order. The NAACP anchored the Memphis protests with such local leaders as Jesse Turner, Benjamin Hooks, Maxine Smith and others playing important roles. The Volunteer Ticket in 1959 was a major voter registration drive which increased the number of Black voters from fewer than 20,000 in 1951 to more than 50,000 in 1959. The desegregation of public facilities and of educational institutions, and the election of Black people to public office soon followed.

The October 3, 1991 election of the former Superintendent of Schools, Dr. Willie W. Herenton, as Memphis' first Black mayor, is one recent outcome of the foundation laid during the Civil Rights Era.

RWB

Rev. King
Support Russell B. Sugarmon Volunteer Candidate for Commissioner of Public Works
Vote for Russell Sugarmon Commissioner of Public Works
HOOK UP with HOOKS as your Juvenile Court JUDGE

Demonstrators in front of 1st National Bank. Signs praise Governors Ross Barnett of MS and George Wallace of AL. Memphis, TN, 1965

Supporters of the Volunteer Ticket welcome Dr. Martin Luther King, Jr. Memphis, TN, March, 1959

Civil rights lawyers Odell Horton, A.W. Willis, Benjamin Hooks, Russell Sugarmon and J.F. Estes at Memphis Police Court after Public Library sit-ins. Memphis, TN, 1960

Odell Sanders, leader of the Brownsville, TN protests

Constance Baker Motley and Thurgood Marshall, NAACP lawyers. Memphis, TN, 1950s

Adam Clayton Powell at Metropolitan Baptist Church. Memphis, TN, 1959

William Edwin Jones pushes daughter Renee Andrewnetta Jones during protest march on Main Street. Memphis, TN, August, 1961

Welfare rights protesters, City Hall. Memphis, TN, 1963

Bus station. Memphis, TN, 1961

Voter Registration and the Tent City Protest
Fayette County, TN, 1960

WHILE MEMPHIS IS URBAN South in Shelby County, Fayette County, which adjoins it, was decidedly more rural in the 1950s, and much like the rural counties of Mississippi which sit on its southern border. Agricultural labor was the main line of employment for Black residents, and most of these worked on the plantations which sent cotton to Memphis.

In the 1950s, Fayette County was one of the 138 counties in the U.S. where Black people outnumbered white people —in Fayette, by two to one. In 1959, young Black residents formed the Fayette County Civic and Welfare League. This came partly in response to rampant disenfranchisement, and partly in response to an off-hand comment by a local judge: "Why, we got nothing against niggers voting. All they gotta do is come to the courthouse and register." If it was so easy, one wonders why only seven-tenths of one percent of all Black people in the county had registered to vote.

White resistance—the all-white primary and activities of the White Citizens Council—strengthened the resolve of this largely spontaneous movement. Local white business leadership circulated a list of all those who registered and sought to deny them loans, fire them from their jobs, and evict them from their homes. As a result of this intimidation, voter registration continued and Tent City—also called Freedom Village—was created. Tent City was built on land made available by a Black landowner to other Black people who had been evicted from their homes for their voter registration activities.

The League filed complaints with the Department of Justice in December 1960. In July, 1962, the department reached an agreement with the white businessmen which blocked them from continuing the practices of economic intimidation.

An article in *Ebony* (September, 1960) and in the *New York Times* (December, 1960) made "Tent City" in Fayette County a widely known struggle. Organizations such as the Student Non-Violent Coordinating Committee (SNCC), the Southern Conference Education Fund (SCEF), the Quaker's Operation Freedom, and the National Baptist Convention under the leadership of Rev. J.H. Jackson rallied national support to the cause. In 1964, the League was strong enough to try to elect two candidates to public office—a local white as Sheriff and a Black minister as tax assessor.

RWB

HERTZ
PACKAGES
HTS FIGHTERS
AFL-CIO
DRINK
Coca-Cola
IN BOTTLES
McFERREN GRO.
OPERATION
"TENT CITY"
SPONSORED BY
RADIO STATION W·H·A·T· PHILA. &
UNIVERSAL AUTO INSURANCE AGENCY. 4211 CHESTNUT ST.
And The People Of Phila.
WHAT

Operation Tent City. Somerville, TN, 1960

Doing laundry at Tent City. Somerville, TN, 1960

Dick Gregory delivers food to farmers. Clarksdale, MS, 1960

Dr. J.H. Jackson, Pres., National Baptist Convention, John McFerren, Fayette County Civic and Welfare League. Somerville, TN, 1960

Tent City, created when Black families were evicted from their homes for voting. Fayette County, TN, 1960

Voter registration. Fayette County, TN, 1960

James Meredith and the Mississippi Campaign
1962 and 1966

HIGHER EDUCATION WAS a key focal point for the struggle over segregation in Mississippi and in most states. Historically, Mississippi colleges were started in the midst of slavery because of the fear that Northern institutions would encourage anti-slavery sentiment among the many white Southern youth who attended these schools. As Mississippi's Governor McNutt stated in 1839: "Those opposed to us in principle, and alienated in interests, can not safely be entrusted with the education of our children." Alcorn University was started in 1871 as a Black college to maintain segregation after slavery was abolished.

James Meredith, a native of Kosciusko, Mississippi and a student at all-Black Jackson State College, sought to end this segregated system just as Medgar Evers, one of his close advisors, and others had done in previous years.

In late 1962, Meredith entered the University of Mississippi under the protection of federal troops. The Governor of Mississippi, Ross Barnett, led the opposition to Meredith's entry on the grounds that it was a state's right, not the federal government's right, to make such decisions. He was joined in his opposition by the leading newspaper in the state, *The Jackson Daily News*, in a story headlined "Ross Risks Jail to Halt Mixing." It editorialized: "We must either submit to the unlawful dictates of the federal government or stand up like men and tell them 'Never!'" Thousands of people gathered to support Governor Barnett's stance. Violence ensued: two people—a French journalist and a salesman—were killed, 28 marshals shot, and 160 marshals wounded. Finally, President John Kennedy ordered more than 23,000 federal troops (three times the population of Oxford) to occupy the campus.

Continuing his campaign in 1966, Meredith organized a "March Against Fear" to prove that a Black man could walk through Mississippi—225 miles from Memphis to Jackson—without being harassed. He wanted to demonstrate his bravery and inspire Black people to register to vote. He started on June 5 and on June 6—only ten miles inside Mississippi—he was wounded in the back by a shotgun blast fired by a Memphis-based racist. Immediately, the entire Civil Rights Movement rallied to continue Meredith's march. Participating were Dr. King of SCLC, Whitney Young of the Urban League, Roy Wilkins of the NAACP, along with two newcomers: Stokely Carmichael of SNCC and Floyd McKissick of CORE.

During the continuation of this march the tension within the movement over "what is to be done" broke out into the open. The NAACP, SCLC, and the Urban League continued to advocate the traditional civil rights agenda. SNCC, CORE, and other young militants had been considerably influenced by Malcolm X, who had been gunned down in February, 1965. Malcolm advocated Black pride, self-determination, and self-defense, and unity with "a global rebellion of the oppressed against the oppressor, the exploited against the exploiter." Before the march ended on June 26th, the leaders of SNCC had called for "Black Power," signalling an important shift in the tactics of the Civil Rights Movement.

RWB

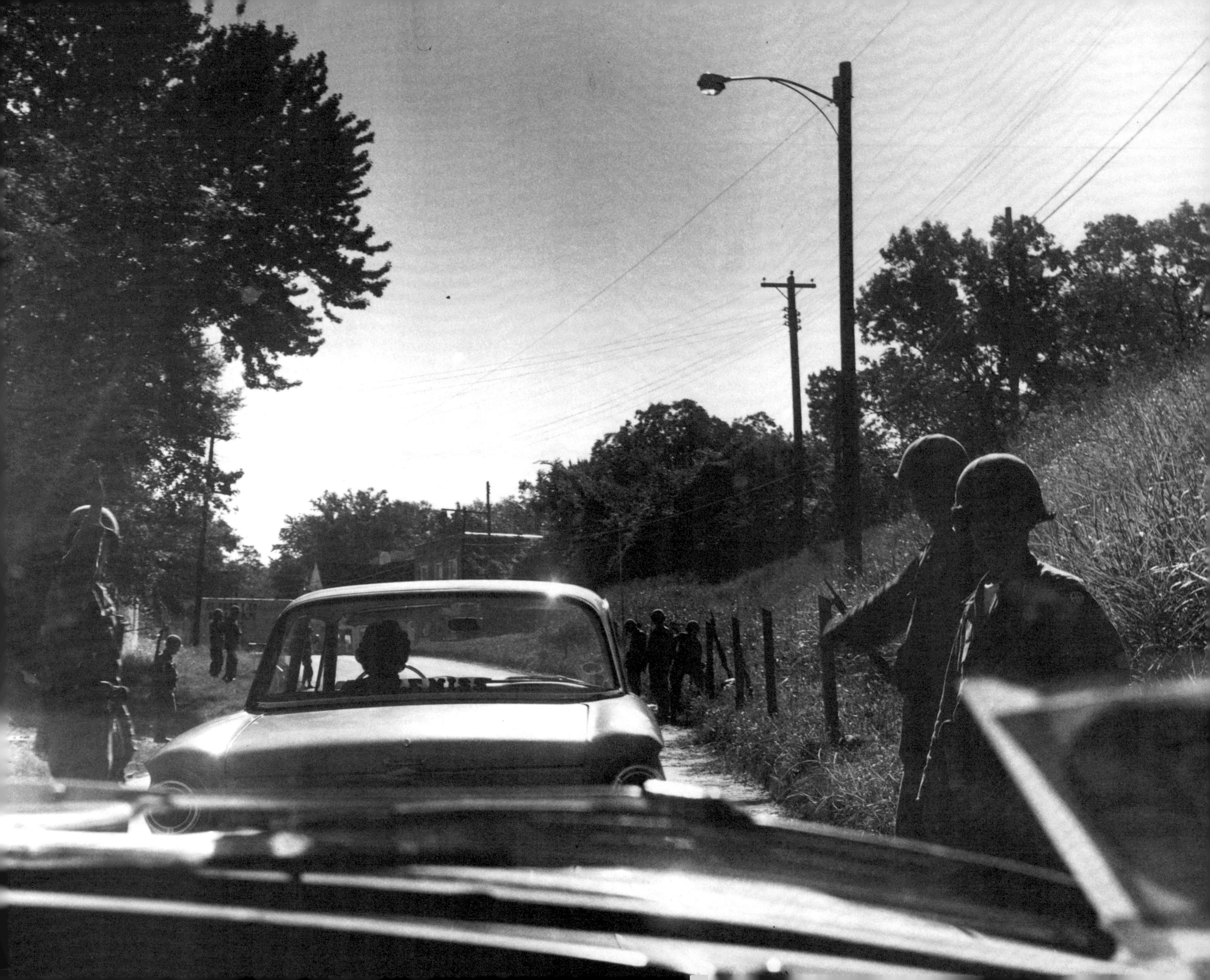

Morning after riots, James Meredith is escorted to University of Mississippi. The National Guard lines the route. Oxford, MS, 1962

FBI agent Bruce Hodges stands behind weapons confiscated from rioters at University of Mississippi following the admission of James Meredith. Oxford, MS, 1962

*Jimmy Hicks, reporter for **New York Amsterdam News**, at University of Mississippi the morning after riots sparked by the admission of James Meredith Oxford, MS, 1962*

Dick Gregory on the porch of James Meredith's family home during the March Against Fear. Kosciusko, MS, 1966

James Meredith returns home to his family after being shot on Highway 51 S. Kosciusko, MS, 1966

James Meredith and family members. Kosciusko, MS, 1966

James Meredith returns to March Against Fear after being shot. Greeted by Rev. Ralph Abernathy. Jackson, MS, 1966

Dr. Martin Luther King, Jr. stops for lunch on the way to a strategy session for March Against Fear. Memphis, TN, 1966

Dr. Martin Luther King, Jr., James Farmer and Rev. Ralph Abernathy. March Against Fear. 1966

March Against Fear, Mississippi Highway 51 S. Coldwater, MS, 1966

Dr. Martin Luther King, Jr., Cleveland Sellers, Bernard Lee, Marvin Scott. March Against Fear, Mississippi Highway 51 S. Coldwater, MS, 1966

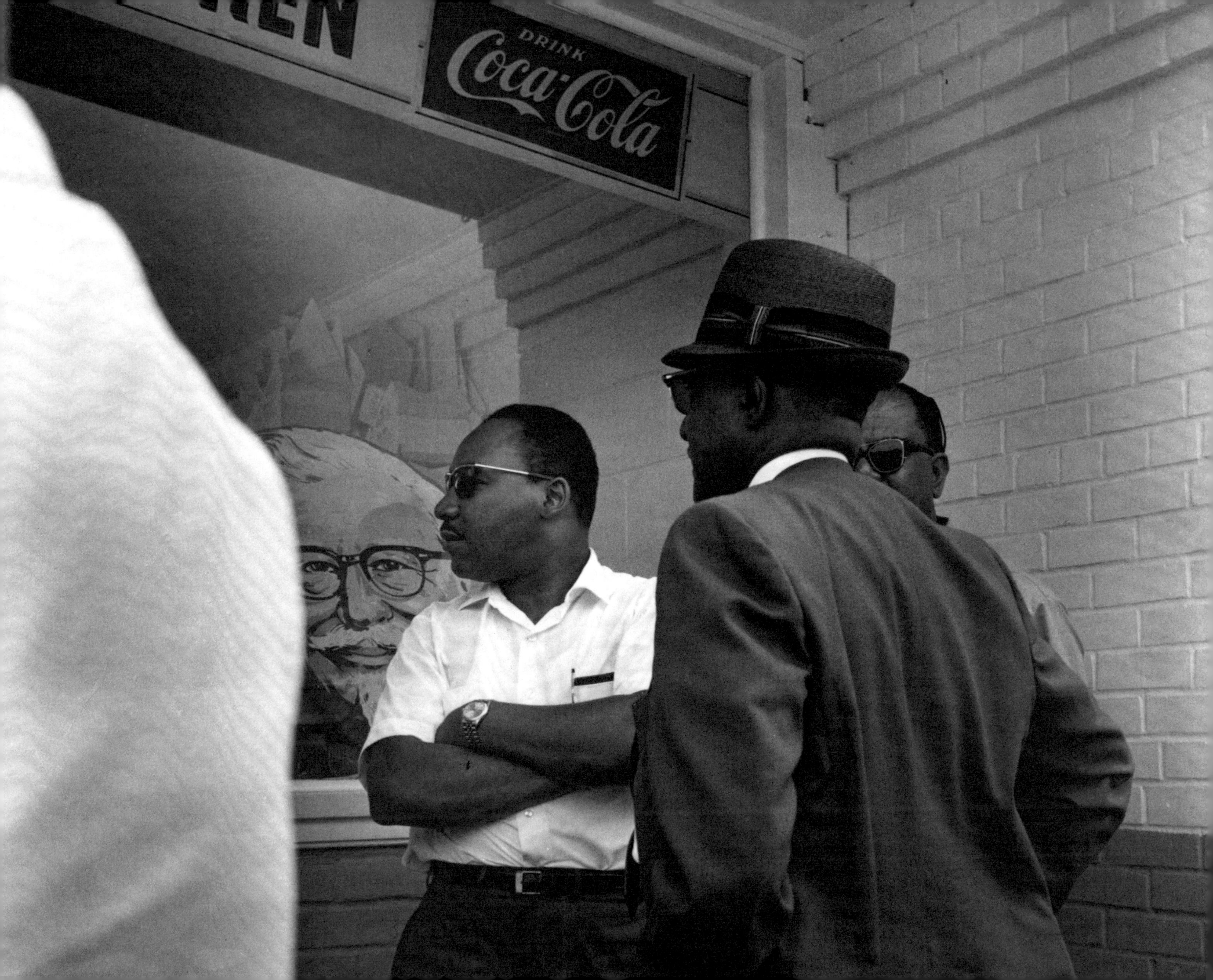
DRINK
Coca-Cola

Dr. Martin Luther King, Jr. standing in doorway of Room 307 and resting in Lorraine Motel following March Against Fear. Memphis, TN, 1966

Medgar Evers
1925-1963

June, 1993 marks the thirtieth anniversary of the death of Medgar Evers. He was born on July 2, 1925 in Decatur, Mississippi to James and Jessie Wright Evers. His father was a stacker in the local sawmill, owned his own land, and was active in the Baptist church. His mother, who had Black and Indian ancestry, did laundry for white families and took in ironing. A devout Christian and leader in the Church of God in Christ, she used her small savings to buy land and build a church. This strong community-building orientation had a profound impact on Medgar.

Medgar was educated in the public schools of Decatur and Newton. He had to walk twelve miles to school and like many Black people developed a deep resentment at seeing white children riding to a nearby segregated school on a bus. He also saw one of his father's friends lynched.

During World War II, he served in the U.S. Army in a segregated field battalion in England and France. Like many other Black veterans, he returned to fight racism at home. After a racial incident, he vowed to his brother, Charles: "When we get out of the Army, we're going to straighten this out."

In 1952, Medgar graduated from Alcorn A & M College (now University). He had married Myrlie Beasley of Vicksburg a year earlier, and went to work for Dr. T.R.M. Howard and the Magnolia Life Insurance Company in Mound Bayou. Following the Brown vs. Board of Education decision, he became the first known Black student to seek admission to the University of Mississippi, applying to the law school in 1954. He became a civil rights leader and the first field secretary of the NAACP in Mississippi during the very difficult times between 1954 and 1963.

With Aaron Henry, Fannie Lou Hamer, Amzie Moore, E.J. Stringer, Winsome Hudson, Susie Ruffin and others, Medgar organized and educated Black Mississippians, especially in the Delta, about their constitutional rights and responsibilities. He investigated countless cases of harassment and brutality, including the murders of George Lee, Lamar Smith, and Emmett Till, all in 1955. He spearheaded campaigns for voting rights, for equal educational opportunity, against brutality, and for desegregation. He counseled James Meredith in his successful bid to enter the University in 1962.

Medgar Evers paid the ultimate price for his steadfastness in the struggle for justice and equality for all Americans regardless of color: he was murdered outside his Jackson home on June 12, 1963. He and Myrlie had three children—Darrell Kenyatta, Reena, and James.

Byron De la Beckwith, an avowed racist, was charged and later twice acquitted by an all-white jury. Evers is buried at Arlington National Cemetery near Washington D.C. Ironically, almost thirty years after his death, Beckwith has been held in a Mississippi prison for almost a year. New evidence of jury tampering has been uncovered. The Mississippi Supreme Court on October 15, 1992 heard final arguments about whether the case should come to trial for a third time.

RWB

Funeral procession for Medgar Evers' Jackson, MS, June, 1963

Mrs. Medgar Evers and family at Medgar Ever's funeral. Jackson, MS, 1963

Funeral march for Medgar Evers. Jackson, MS, June, 1963

Dr. Martin Luther King, Jr. is stopped by police at Medgar Evers' Funeral. Jackson, MS, June, 1963

Montgomery Bus Boycott
Montgomery, AL, 1955

NO PERSON HAS come to symbolize the aspirations of Black people for civil rights in the U.S. more than Dr. Martin Luther King, Jr.

But so much attention is often devoted to Dr. King that we sometimes forget that a social movement which was not initiated by Dr. King was successfully launched in Montgomery and provided the platform on which he entered into a brilliant career of social activism. As SCLC staff member Ella Baker put it, "the Movement made Martin rather than Martin making the Movement."

On December 1, 1955, Rosa Parks, a seamstress and NAACP activist, refused to give up her seat on a Montgomery bus to a white man. She was arrested for violating the local segregation ordinance.

There are key points about the Montgomery Bus Boycott which are not covered in most presentations. First, this was not the first bus protest in Montgomery. And Mrs. Parks was not the first person to be arrested for refusing to give up her seat for a white person—two Black women had been previously arrested. One of them was Claudette Colvin, a fifteen-year-old student, had been dragged from a bus and charged with assault and battery when she refused to move.

Professor JoAnn Robinson, Professor of English at Alabama State University and head of the Women's Political Council, represented the women during negotiations with the bus company, a year before the Bus Boycott. It was Professor Robinson who called together local leaders to discuss building support for this movement. Among those who responded were E.D. Nixon, a pullman car porter and NAACP president, and a local minister and activist in the Baptist Ministers Alliance, Rev. Ralph David Abernathy. Abernathy played a key role in organizing the Montgomery Improvement Association which led the local struggle.

Second, Rosa Parks did not refuse to give up her seat simply because she was tired. She had a long history as a key leader in the NAACP, and had attended political education classes sponsored by civil rights organizers in the South. She had also been moved to action by the brutal murder of young Emmett Till in Mississippi just several months before, in September 1955. But E.D. Nixon, Rev. Abernathy, and others felt that Rosa Parks had the stature that would rally mass support for a successful boycott. Rev. Abernathy also suggested that his friend, Rev. King, who was busy completing his doctoral dissertation and pastoring Dexter Avenue Baptist Church, be called on to involve himself in the developing struggle.

This boycott achieved success after 381 days. The Southern Christian Leadership Conference (SCLC) was formed in January, 1957, with Dr. King as president.

The success of the boycott and the leadership abilities of Dr. King catapulted him to international stature, and SCLC became Dr. King's base for more than a decade of civil rights leadership. SCLC led the confrontation over segregation in Birmingham, led the Selma to Montgomery March and was active in many other campaigns. Dr. King was awarded the Nobel Peace Prize in December, 1964.

RWB

*Dr. Martin Luther King, Jr.
in front of desegragated bus.
Montgomery, AL, 1956*

Dr. Martin Luther King, Jr. and Rev. Ralph Abernathy on first desegragated bus. Montgomery, AL, 1956

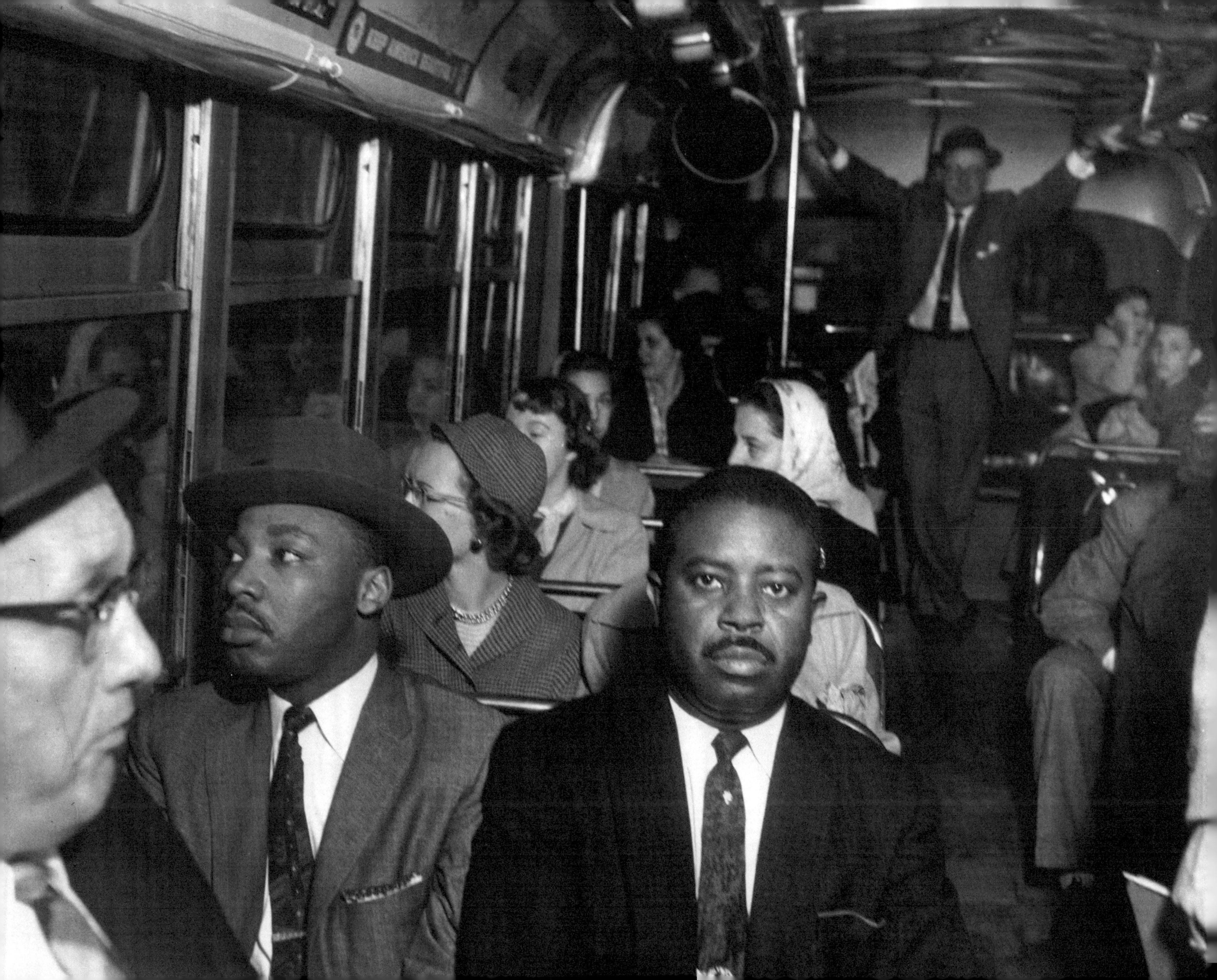

Dr. Martin Luther King, Jr. at conclusion of march in support of bus boycott. Montgomery, AL, 1956

Sanitation Workers' Strike
Memphis, TN, 1968

On February 1, 1968, two Black garbage workers—Echol Cole and Robert Walker—were killed when they were sucked into a faulty garbage packer. The deaths were a spark: by February 12th, 930 out of 1,100 sanitation workers went out on strike, along with most of the street repair crews. Only 38 of approximately 200 trucks could be put on the streets to collect the 5,000,000 pounds of garbage the city produced each day. For four years, AFSCME—the American Federation of State, County, and Municipal Employees—had been attempting to build its Local 1733 among the mostly Black sanitation workers, led by T.O. Jones. Jones, a garbageman since 1959, was fired for leading a walkout of workers in 1963. He formed the Independent Workers Association in 1964, which later merged with AFSCME. Jones served as the local's president.

The national office of AFSCME, under the leadership of Jerry Wurf, saw the importance of the Memphis struggle and sent in a number of its top organizers. They included P.C. Ciampa, field services director and Bill Lucy, a native of Memphis who would go on to become president of the Coalition of Black Trade Unionists and the national AFSCME treasurer.

Urban rebellions had swept across the U.S. in 1967, and a new mood was evident throughout the nation. There were 164 disorders with more than 100 in July alone, the most serious occurring in Detroit and Newark. The National Commission on Civil Disorders was appointed by President Johnson and, given its conservative membership drawn from the power structure, brought back a report on March 1, 1968 with startling conclusions: "Our nation is moving toward two societies, one black, one white—separate and unequal."

Based on his observations in the rural community of Marks in Quitman County, Mississippi, Dr. King had already made his controversial decision to shift tactics by focusing on poverty and class issues, in addition to issues of racial discrimination. He was organizing a Poor People's Campaign and thought that Memphis represented a key battle in this regard. He came to Memphis on March 18th and addressed an enthusiastic rally at Mason Temple. He was invited back to lead a second march on City Hall.

The Memphis Sanitation Workers' strike was important in U.S. history because it represented the powerful dynamics of race and class and the possibility of an effective coalition between organized labor and the Civil Rights Movement. Many different organizations supported the strike. There was Community on the Move for Equality, or C.O.M.E., the Black community movement which was formed to support the strike, with Rev. James Lawson as chairman. There was the NAACP, historically the key force in civil rights efforts in Memphis. And there were new organizations, including the Black Organizing Project (BOP), a group of young militants also known as "The Invaders." Local ministers and union locals from around the U.S. were also supportive. Tension had been growing among these local organizations about how best to wage the struggle.

Dr. King flew into Memphis to lead another march on March 28th. Growing frustration and anger at the city's slow response to the strike and the actions of police at a previous march led to violence on this march. A sixteen year-old boy, Larry Payne, was killed. This would also be Dr. King's last march. On April 4, 1968, Dr. King was assassinated.

RWB

Sanitation Workers' strike, Main Street. Memphis, TN, 1968

Natinal Guard at City Hall. Memphis, TN, 1968

Sanitation Workers' march is stopped on Main Street. Memphis, TN, 1968

Dr. Martin Luther King Jr.'s last march, Memphis Sanitation Workers' strike. T.O. Jones, Bishop B. Julien. Memphis, TN, March 28, 1968

March in solidarity with Sanitation Workers, Hernando Street. Memphis, TN, March 28, 1968

Dr. Martin Luther King Jr.'s last press conference, after strategy meeting at Centenary United Methodist Church. Memphis, TN, April 3, 1968

Rev. L.R. Donson, Leader of the Baptist Minister's Association, at Main and Madison Street, at height of Sanitation Workers' strike. Memphis, TN, March 1968

Mother of Larry Payne arrives at her son's funeral. Payne was killed during Sanitation Workers' march. Memphis, TN, March 28, 1968

Fannie Lou Hamer addresses striking Sanitation Workers. Memphis, TN, 1968

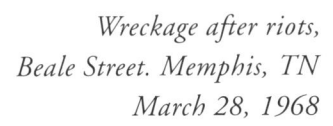

Wreckage after riots, Beale Street. Memphis, TN March 28, 1968

The Assassination of Dr. Martin Luther King, Jr.
April 4, 1968

On April 4, 1968, on the fifty-third day of the Memphis Sanitation Workers' strike, Dr. Martin Luther King, Jr. was shot and killed at the Lorraine Motel on the balcony outside his room. James Earl Ray was arrested and convicted of the murder, but there is still considerable discussion about who was responsible for the assassination.

The murder of Dr. King led to rebellions in the streets of Memphis and in over one hundred and twenty-five cities throughout the United States. Seven hundred fires were set in Washington, D.C., and twenty blocks on Chicago's West Side went up in flames. By the end of the week, 21,000 federal troops and 34,000 National Guardsmen had been called out in a hundred cities to stop the rebellions. Forty-six were left dead, more than 3,000 were injured, and over 25,000 were arrested. Property damage was estimated at almost $50 million. Dr. King's death also led to a decisive escalation of the militancy of the Black Liberation movement. If non-violent Rev. King could be killed, was nothing sacred?

Another march in honor of Dr. King and his family was held in Memphis on April 8th. Dr. King's body was taken to Atlanta, where his funeral services (the largest funeral for a private citizen in U.S. history), were held.

The struggle of the Memphis Sanitation Workers continued. There were three main demands. One involved a wage increase and a second involved a dues check-off in which the city would deduct union dues from workers' checks. The third, and most important, involved a demand for city recognition of AFSCME, AFL-CIO, Local 1733 as the designated representative for certain employees within the Division of Public Works. But the demand for recognition was more fundamental than the union, as the bold statement of the many "I AM A MAN" signs in the strike made clear. It was a matter of basic dignity.

On Tuesday, April 16th, sixty-five days after the strike began and twelve days after Dr. King's death, the workers returned to work having won all of their demands — union recognition, the pay increase, and the dues check-off. They had also won recognition of their manhood!

SCLC held its annual convention in Memphis in July, 1968 with Dr. King's closest associate and friend, Rev. Ralph D. Abernathy, presiding.

The untimely death of Dr. Martin Luther King, Jr. had a significant impact on the nation and on the freedom struggle of Black people. For example, a generation of college students were radicalized in its wake, and sought to change the policies and practices of institutional racism through social protest and disruption of universities. These actions, along with the general national concern about racism, contributed to a dramatic result: between 1960 and 1970, the number of Black students enrolled in colleges increased from 99,000 to 417,000; it increased to 666,000 in 1975. Black Studies programs and courses were also institutionalized on many campuses.

In 1983, the U.S. Congress and the President passed and signed legislation which recognized the contributions of Dr. Martin Luther King, Jr. by establishing January 15th, his birthday, as a federal holiday. Beginning in 1986, it is the first such honor ever accorded to an African-American citizen.

RWB

Lorraine Motel after assassination of Dr. Martin Luther King, Jr. Memphis, TN, April, 1968

Andrew Young, Bernard Lee and Hosea Williams, Room 307, Lorraine Motel. Memphis, TN, April 5, 1968

Maxine Smith, Memphis NAACP, Leroy Clark and H. Ralph Jackson marching on Main Street to press conference after King assassination. Memphis, TN, 1968

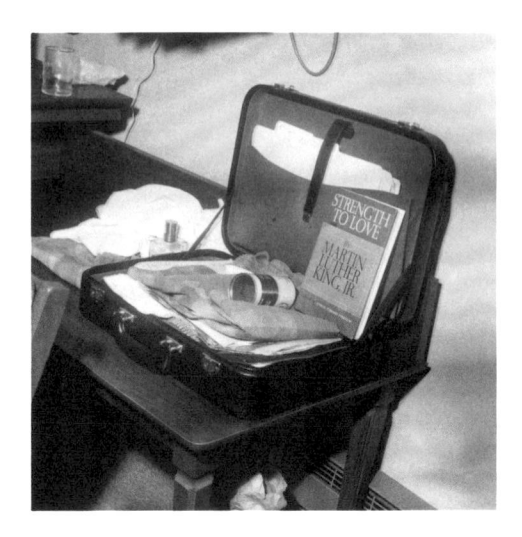

Briefcase of Dr. Martin Luther King, Jr., Room 306, Lorraine Motel. Memphis, TN, April, 1968

Boarding house bathroom window from which James Earl Ray shot and killed Dr. Martin Luther King Jr. Memphis, TN, April, 1968

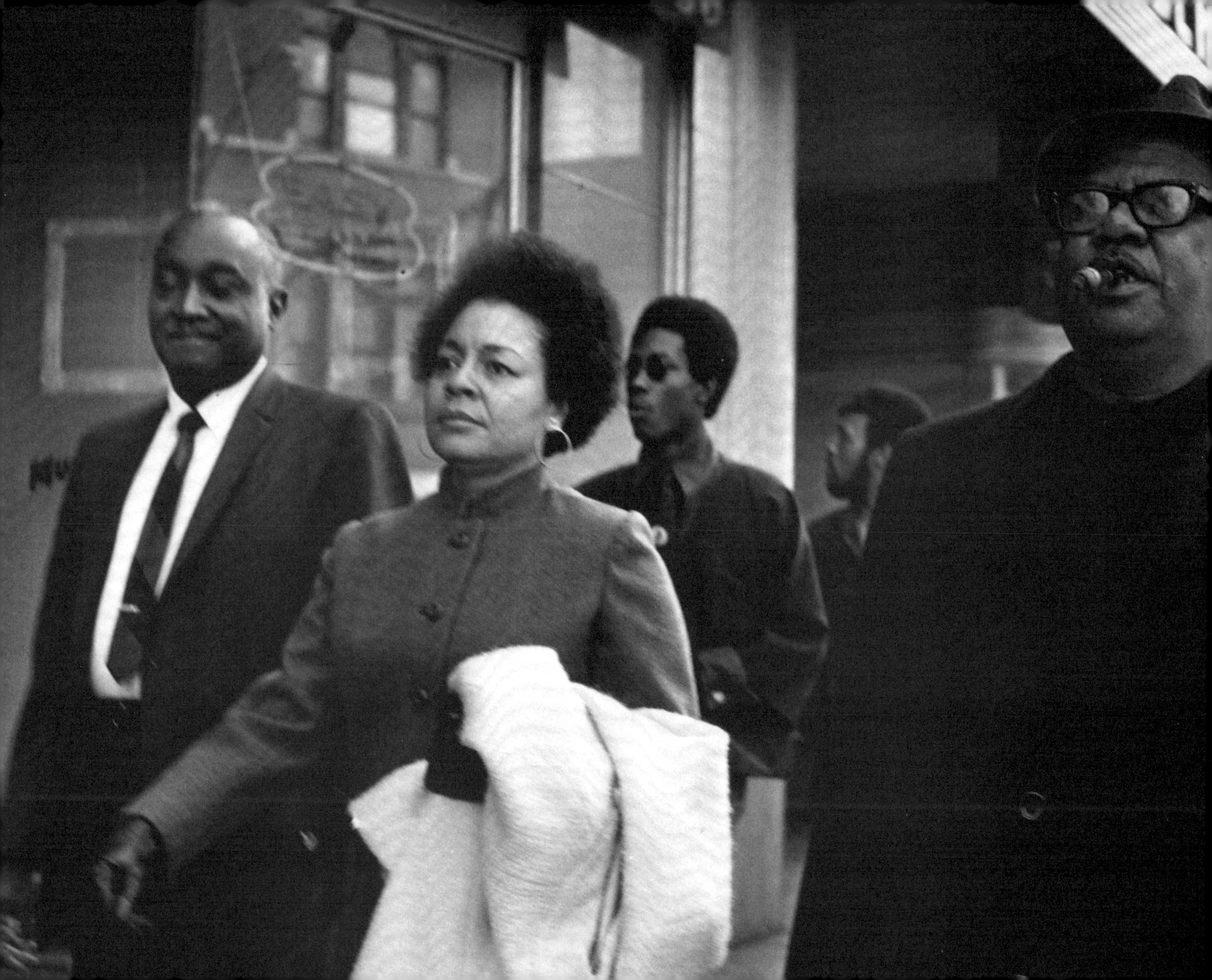

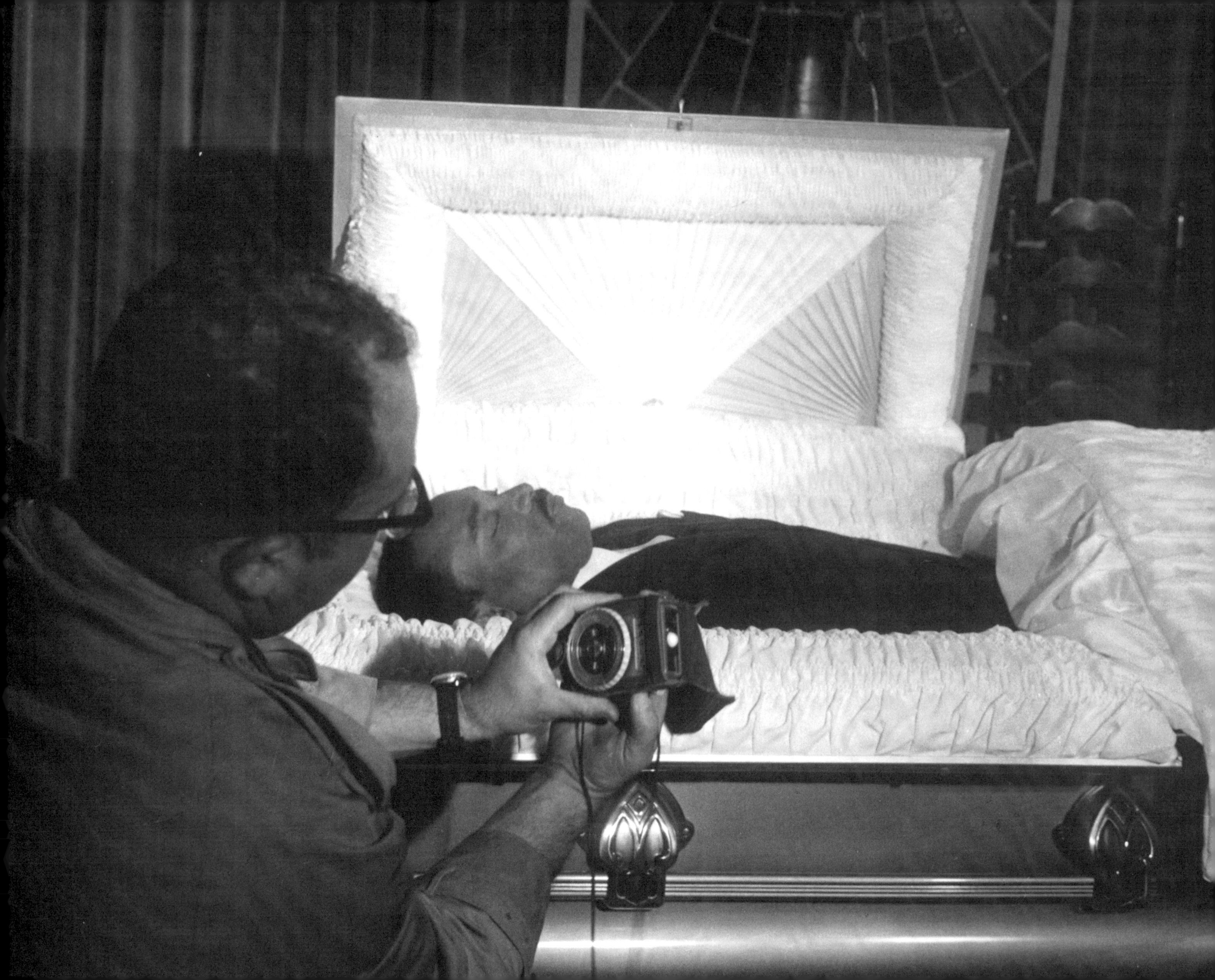

Dr. Martin Luther King, Jr. lies in state at R.S. Lewis funeral home. Memphis, TN, 1968

Bishop Jordan, AME Baptist Church, T.O. Jones, Head of Sanitation Workers, Walter Reuther, United Auto Workers, lead protest march. Memphis, TN, April 8, 1968

Marchers on Main Street after assassination of Dr. Martin Luther King, Jr. Memphis, TN, 1968

Protest march. Memphis, TN, April 8, 1968

National Guard at Main and Linden Street after assassination of Dr. Martin Luther King, Jr. Memphis, TN, 1968

Lorraine Motel after the assassination of Dr. Martin Luther King, Jr. Memphis, TN, 1968

Beale Street after riots following the assassination of Dr. Martin Luther King, Jr. Memphis, TN, 1968

Son of Rev. Ralph Abernathy rides on the back of press truck after assassination of Dr. Martin Luther King, Jr. Memphis, TN, 1968

Funeral procession for Dr. Martin Luther King, Jr. on Auburn Street after leaving M.L. King's church. Atlanta, GA, April, 1968

Coretta Scott King and Martin Luther King, Sr., Dr. King's funeral procession. Atlanta, GA, April, 1968

Coretta Scott King addresses SCLC Convention. Memphis, TN, July, 1968

Rev. Ralph Abernathy kisses Dr. King's daughter at SCLC Convention Rally, Club Paradise. Memphis, TN, July, 1968

Rosa Parks, Rev. Ralph Abernathy and King family at Mason Temple, SCLC Convention. Memphis, TN, July, 1968

Bayard Rustin at Mason Temple. Memphis, TN, 1968

Poor People's Campaign
Marks, MS, 1968

The escalation of the Vietnam war, the urban rebellions and the emergence of "Black Power," and the increasingly negative response SCLC's program met with in cities like Chicago put considerable strain on the civil rights leadership of Dr. Martin Luther King, Jr. In February, 1967, he abandoned his position of support for the war, and he began to articulate a new program of action that addressed the deepening crisis of Black people in the cities. This was the Poor People's Campaign.

The aim of the Campaign was to "raise to a level of visibility the problem of poverty in this country." The plan was to bring thousands of poor people to Washington, house them in shanties, conduct large rallies and demonstrations, and then settle down for a long-term non-violent campaign with civil disobedience and mass arrests. Eventually, a nationwide boycott would be called. In building the campaign Dr. King sought to achieve success with several new tactics: the national boycott, building a "rainbow coalition" of poor people of various ethnic groups, and developing an explicit position on the need to abolish poverty.

There was much discussion of Dr. King's increasingly radical posture on international and domestic issues. "Something is wrong with capitalism as it now stands in the United States. We are not interested in being integrated into this value structure. Power must be relocated, a radical redistribution of power must take place. We must do something to these men to change them," he said. The FBI escalated its spying on Dr. King, and launched plans to actively disrupt the Campaign.

Marks, Mississippi was one of the main staging areas from which poor people were to travel to Washington, D.C. The kickoff date was to have been April 22nd, but Dr. King's assassination led to a one week postponement until April 28, 1968. There was considerable debate about the feasibility of having such a march at that particular time. But most SCLC staffers felt it was an appropriate way to honor Dr. King and his commitment to racial and economic justice in the United States.

The death of Dr. King and the rebellions which followed also crystallized another reaction which had been growing: that of a "white backlash" against the civil rights gains of the 1960s. In 1968 Richard Nixon was elected U.S. president and "law and order," not justice and equality, became the key issue in U.S. politics.

As conditions for many Black people worsened, the issues of building a mass movement to continue the struggle and the role of leadership were also forced to the forefront in the wake of Dr. King's assassination. As SNCC activist Diane Nash said, "If people think that it was Martin Luther King's movement, then today they—young people—are more like to say, 'gosh, I wish we had a Martin Luther King here today to lead us.'... If people knew how that movement started, then the question they would ask themselves is, 'What can I do?'"

RWB

Mule Train, Poor People's March on Washington, D.C., 1968

Rev. Jesse Jackson at Resurrection City. Washington, D.C., 1968

Poor People's Camp. Marks, MS, 1968

Poor People's Camp. Marks, MS, 1968

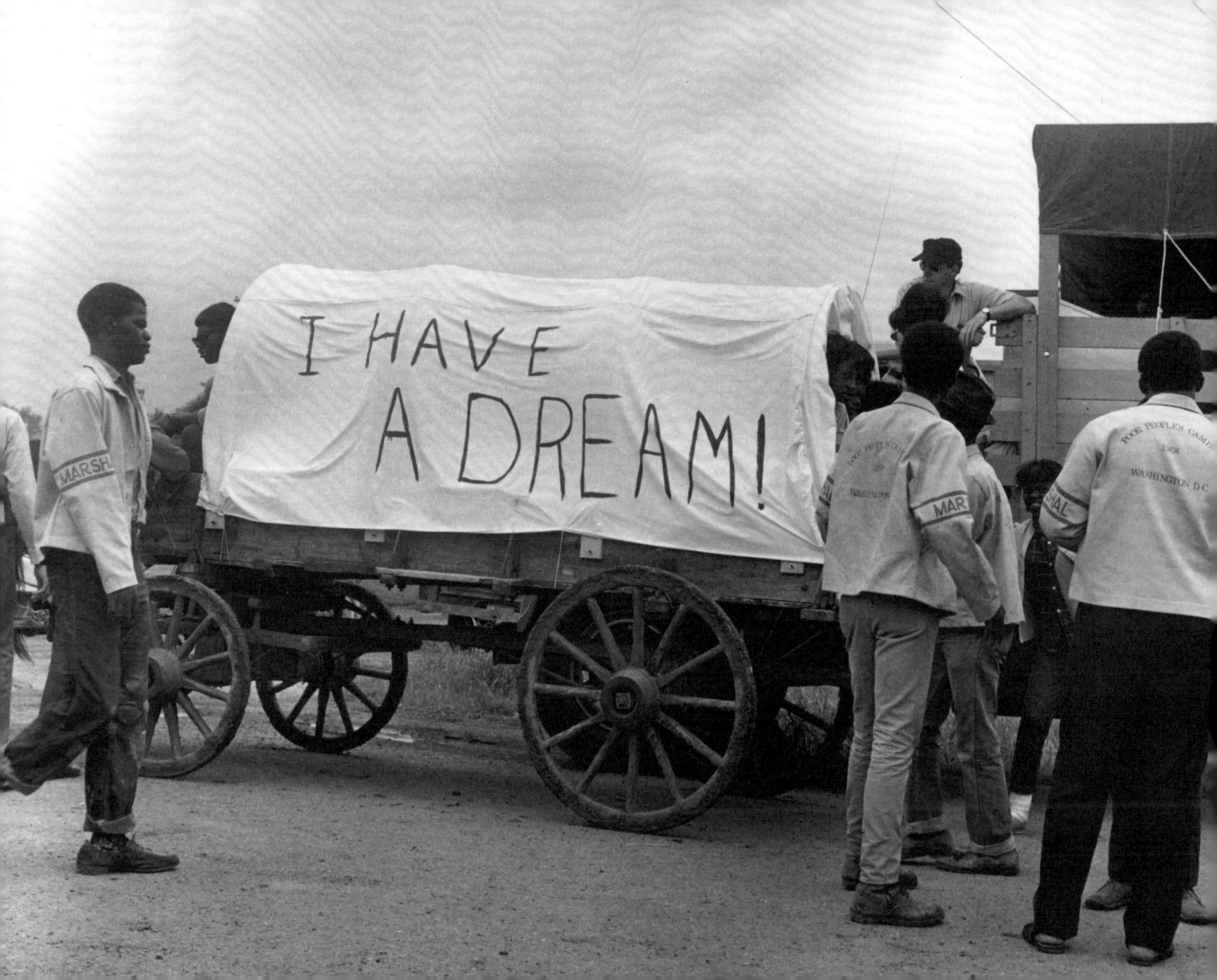
I HAVE
A DREAM!
MARSHA
1968
WASHINGTON, D.C.

Poor People's March to Washington, D.C., 1968

Afterword

["A Picture is Worth A Thousand Words": A Modest Proposal for a Database of African-American Documentary Photographers]

The tremendous attention to the history of photography in the century and a half since its inception still leaves me worried that not enough attention is being paid to Black photographers. With a few rare exceptions, a more comprehensive survey leaves me no less worried.

For example, more recently, *Documentary Photography* (Boston: Focal Press, 1989), by the noted Farm Security Administration (FSA) photographer Arthur Rothstein contains almost no information about this rich tradition of Black photographers, though billed as "a history of documentary photography to the present." Except for two photographs by Gordon Parks, no Black photographers are included. There is a substantial body of work on the FSA photographers, but similar attention has not been devoted to Black photographers.

There are rare exceptions. The work of Deborah Willis-Thomas, former curator of Photography at the Schomburg Center for Research in Black Culture of the New York Public Library, and now with the Smithsonian initiative to develop the National African-American Museum, deserves special mention. Her *Black Photographers, 1840-1940: An Illustrated Bio-bibliography* (Garland Publishing, 1985) and her second installment, *An Illustrated Bio-bibliography of Black Photographers, 1940-1988* (Garland Publishing, 1989), present the most comprehensive look at Black photographers thus far published in the U.S. Along with Schomburg director Howard Dodson, Willis-Thomas edited *Black Photographers Bear Witness: 100 Years of Social Protest,* a catalogue from a 1989 exhibit which she curated at the Williams College Museum of Art.[17]

Other important works include Jeanne Moutoussamy-Ashe, *Viewfinders: Black Women Photographers* (Dodd-Mead, 1986), James Alinder (editor), *Roy DeCarava: Photographs* (The Friends of Photography, 1981), and Valencia Hollis Coar's *A Century of Black Photographers, 1840-1968* (Rhode Island School of Design, Museum of Art, 1983). Moreover, books which present historical photography focused on the Black experience are also useful, including such works as *A True Likeness: The Black South of Richard Samuel Roberts, 1920-1936* (University of South Carolina Press). A recent publication is *Songs for My People— African-Americans: A Self-Portrait* (edited by Easter, Cheers, and Brooks; Little-Brown, 1992), a selection of photographs from thousands taken by fifty Black photographers in 1990.

Civil rights has been the particular subject of several works. John Tweedle's *A Lasting Impression: A Collection of Photographs of Martin Luther King, Jr.* (edited by Hermene D. Hartman, University of South Carolina Press, 1983) focuses on Dr. Martin Luther King, Jr. and on his many visits to Chicago. Tweedle was the first Black photographer to work at a major metropolitan daily. Another example is *Powerful Days: The Civil Rights Photography of Charles Moore* (Stewart, Tabori, and Chang, 1991). Moore is a white Alabama native who covered some of the most significant battles in the civil rights struggle.

The Black Photographers' Annual is another rare exception. In its 1973 edition, writer Clayton Riley observed in his introduction:

"The nation is surrounded by images of what it is supposed to be. And it becomes institutionally and individually what those images imply, what they indicate, what they impose. The Black visual artist, his work for many years denied a true and complete public, develops muscle and emotional determination through a years-long struggle simply to be, exist and work."

Riley continues after describing some of the images which appear in the volume:

"A collection, then, of the works of Black photographers, a monumental testament both to their enormous gifts, and to the people from whom they have come, the people, wondrous and strong, who have been their subjects for this study of life."

But it is still the case that the work of Black photographers like Withers is generally "invisible" when an overview of photography in the U.S. is considered. This theme of invisibility is a key concept that Black writers have often used to capture the essence of the lack of access and equity in many institutions and aspects of U.S. society. As Ralph Ellison exclaimed in *Invisible Man*, "I am invisible, understand, simply because people refuse to see me.... When they approach me they see only my surroundings, themselves, or figments of their imagination—indeed, everything and anything except me."

It is in full recognition of the power of this tradition of documentary photography among African-American photographers and the importance of the Black experience which has been central to their work that I venture this proposal for a National Center for African-American Documentary Photography.

The idea would be to use the most recent advances in electronic imaging, digital storage, computer databases, and video to insure that the images of Black photographers and their tremendous reservoir of knowledge as community scribes—griots, as my friend Doug Harris calls his video company—is not lost to future generations.[18] While there are excellent sources available, we are greatly in need of additional sources—African-American sources—of images of what this nation is supposed to be.[19]

My relationship with several photographers who have aided my work over the past two decades convinces me of the need for such a project. One example is the late Tony Rhoden, a Chicago photographer who operated Rhoden Photo Service on the South Side. The late T.A. Armstrong took many pictures of Black life in Jackson, Mississippi, and permitted us to use important photographs of Medgar Evers. "Younger" photographers include Doug Harris of New York City, Robert Jones of Memphis, and Roy Lewis and Roland Freeman, both of Washington, D.C., and Bobby Sengstacke of Chicago. In fact, in an earlier period, the photographs of Robert Van Lierop recorded during his visit behind the lines with FRELIMO, the liberation movement in Mozambique, should be included in such an effort as well, since they helped to fuel the Africa support movement in the U.S. during the early 1970s. The list of important Black photographers who should be included in such a project is clearly much longer than these few names.

Finally, it would be a monumentally valuable contribution if a selection of photographs from one of the most important archives on the Black experience in the world—that of Mr. John H. Johnson and Johnson Publications in Chicago—could be included as a part of this project. One need only to peruse the pages of *Jet*, *Ebony*, and *Negro Digest/Black World* to understand the seminal nature of Mr. Johnson's collection. Similarly, the photo files of leading African-American newspapers such as the *Chicago Defender*, the *Pittsburgh Courier*, the *Baltimore Afro-American*, the *Jackson Advocate*, and the *Atlanta Daily World*, among others, could also lend valuable sources for such an effort.

In my mind, the photographs of Ernest C. Withers are one good place to begin such a documentation project. And I am pleased to report that Mr. Withers is vitally interested in this idea, and he has pledged his full support.

RWB

Selective Bibliography

The following titles are among those which are useful in understanding Black History and interpreting the history of the Civil Rights Movement and the photographs of Ernest C. Withers.

General Reference and Historical Background

Alkalimat, Abdul and Associates. *Introduction to Afro-American Studies: A Peoples College Primer (1984).* Available from 21st Century Books and Publications, P.O. Box 803351, Chicago, IL 60680.

Aptheker, Herbert. *A Documentary History of the Negro People in the United States: From Colonial Times to the Civil War.* (The Citadel Press, 1968).

Bunche, Ralph J. *The Political Status of the Negro in the Age of FDR.* (University of Chicago Press, 1973).

DuBois, W.E.B. *Black Reconstruction in America: An Essay toward a History of the Part Which Black Folk Played in the Attempt to Reconstruct Democracy in America, 1860-1880.* (Athenaeum, 1935, 1975).

Davis, Allison, Burleigh Gardner, and Mary Gardner (with St. Clair Drake). *Deep South: A Social Anthropological Analysis of Caste and Class.* (UCLA Center for Afro-American Studies, 1941, 1988).

Foster, William Z. *The Negro People in American History.* (International Publishers, 1954, 1973).

Grossman, James R. *Land of Hope: Chicago, Black Southerners, and the Great Migration.* (The University of Chicago Press, 1989).

Jones, Jacqueline. *Labor of Love, Labor of Sorrow: Black Women, Work and the Family, From Slavery to the Present.* (Vintage Books, 1986).

Lewinson, P. *Race Class and Party: A History of Negro Suffrage and White Politics in the South.* (New York: Grosset & Dunlap, 1932).

Marks, Carole. *Farewell—We're Good and Gone: The Great Black Migration.* (Indiana University Press, 1989).

McMillen, Neil R. *Dark Journey: Black Mississippians in the Age of Jim Crow.* (University of Illinois Press, 1989).

Sigafoos, Robert A. *Cotton Row To Beale Street: A Business History of Memphis.* (Memphis State University Press, 1992).

Wilson, Charles R. and Williams Ferris, eds. *The Encyclopedia of Southern Culture* (University of North Carolina Press, 1989).

THE CIVIL RIGHTS ERA

Abernathy, Ralph D. *And the Walls Came Tumbling Down: An Autobiography.* (Harper and Row, 1989).

Bailey, Ronald W. *Remembering Medgar Evers... For a New Generation (1983).* Available from The Afro Scholar Press, P.O., Box 190742, Roxbury, MA 02119.

Bates, Daisy. *The Long Shadow of Little Rock: A Memoir.* (David McKay Company, 1963).

Beifuss, Joan Turner. *At the River I Stand: Memphis, the 1968 Strike, and Martin Luther King.* (Carlson Publishing, 1989).

Branch, Taylor. *Parting the Waters: America in the King Years 1954-63.* (Simon & Schuster Inc. New York, 1988).

Carmichael, Stokely and Charles Hamilton, *Black Power: The Politics of Liberation in America.* (Random House, 1967).

Carson, Clayborne. *In the Struggle: SNCC and the Black Awakening of the 1960's.* (Harvard University, 1981)

Carson, Clayborne, *The Papers of Martin Luther King Jr., Volume I.* (University of California Press, 1992).

Carson, Clayborne, David J. Garrow, Vincent Harding, Darlene Clark Hine. *Eyes On The Prize: America's Civil Rights Years.* (Penguin Books, 1987).

Crawford, Vicki, Jacqueline Rouse, Barbara Woods. *Women in the Civil Rights Movement: Trailblazers and Torchbearers, 1941-1965.* (Carlson Publishing, 1990).

Eagles, Charles (ed.), *The Civil Rights Movement in America.* (University Press of Mississippi, 1986).

Evers, Mrs. Medgar (Myrlie) with William Peters. *For Us, The Living.* (Doubleday, 1967).

Fager, Charles. *Uncertain Resurrection: The Poor People's Washington Campaign.* (William B. Eerdmans Publishing Company, 1969).

Fayette County Project Volunteers. *Step By Step: Evolution and Operation of the Cornell Students' Civil Rights Project in Tennessee, Summer, 1964.* (W.W. Norton & Company Inc., 1965).

Garrow, David J. (editor). *Martin Luther King, Jr. and the Civil Rights Movement (a series of 18 volumes).* (Carlson Publishing Company).

Gitlin, Todd. *The Sixties: Years of Hope, Days of Rage.* (Bantam, 1987).

Hampton, Henry and Steve Fayer, *Voices of the Civil Rights Movement: An Oral History of the Civil Rights Movement from the 1950s to the 1980s.* (Bantam, 1990).

McMillen, Neil. *The Citizens' Council: Organized Resistance to the Second Reconstruction.* (Univ. of Illinois Press, 1971).

Meredith, James. *Three Years in Mississippi.* (Indiana Univ. Press, 1966).

Moody, Anne. *Coming of Age In Mississippi.* (Dial Press Inc., 1968).

Parker, Frank R. *Black Votes Count: Polical Empowerment in Mississippi after 1965.* (University of North Carolina Press, 1990).

Raines, Howell (ed.). *My Soul is Rested: The Story of the Civil Rights Movements in the Deep South.* (Putnam, 1977).

Robinson, Jo Ann. *The Montgomery Bus Boycott and the Women who Started It: The Memoir of Jo Ann Gibson Robinson.* (University of Tennessee Press, 1987).

Whitfield Stephen J. *A Death In the Delta: The Story of Emmett Till.* (The Free Press, 1988).

Youth of the Rural Organizing Culture Center, Holmes County, MS. *Minds Stayed on Freedom: The Civil Rights Struggle in the Rural South.* (Westview, 1991).

DATE DUE

NOV 0 1 ENT'D			

Demco

SCHOOL OF THE MUSEUM
OF FINE ARTS - BOSTON

TUFTS UNIVERSITY LIBRARIES
3 9090 01743 2572